The
Believer's
Full Blessing
of Pentecost

D1113878

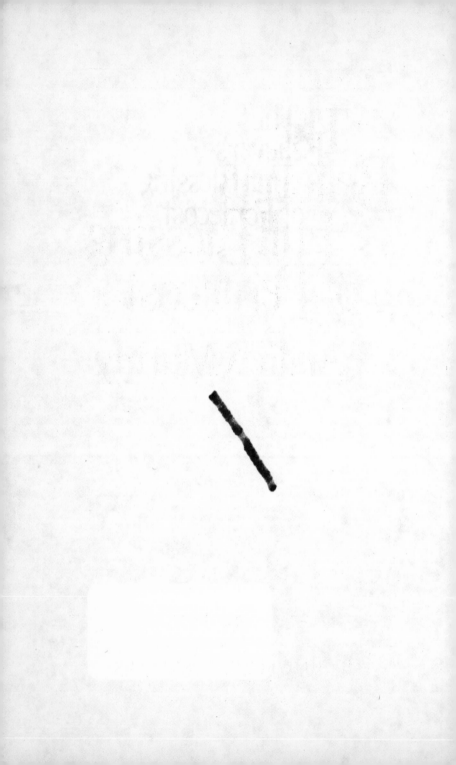

The Believer's Full Blessing of Pentecost

Andrew Murray

BETHANY HOUSE PUBLISHERS
MINNEAPOLIS, MINNESOTA 55438
A Division of Bethany Fellowship, Inc.

Copyright © 1984
Bethany House Publishers
All Rights Reserved

Published by Bethany House Publishers
A Division of Bethany Fellowship, Inc.
6820 Auto Club Road, Minneapolis, MN 55438

Printed in the United States of America

Library of Congress Cataloging in Publication Data

Murray, Andrew, 1818-1917.
   The believer's full blessing of Pentecost.

   Rev. ed. of: The full blessing of Pentecost. 1974.
   1. Holy Spirit. I. Murray, Andrew, 1828-1917.
Full blessing of Pentecost.   II. Title.
BT121.M85 1984   234'.1   84-12301
ISBN 0-87123-597-8

Other Books by Andrew Murray

ANDREW MURRAY CHRISTIAN
MATURITY LIBRARY
The Believer's Secret of Obedience
The Believer's Call to Commitment
The Believer's Secret of a Perfect Heart
The Believer's New Life
The Believer's Secret of Holiness
The Believer's Full Blessing of Pentecost
The Believer's New Covenant
The Spirit of Christ

ANDREW MURRAY PRAYER LIBRARY
The Believer's School of Prayer
The Ministry of Intercessory Prayer
The Secret of Believing Prayer
The Believer's Prayer Life

ANDREW MURRAY DEVOTIONAL LIBRARY
Daily Secrets of Christian Living
The Believer's Daily Renewal
Day by Day with Andrew Murray

How to Raise Your Children for Christ
The Master's Indwelling
Like Christ
Money
Jesus Christ: Prophet-Priest

ANDREW MURRAY was born in South Africa in 1828. After receiving his education in Scotland and Holland, he returned to that land and spent many years there as both pastor and missionary. He was a staunch advocate of biblical Christianity. He is best known for his many devotional books.

Contents

Introduction

The message which this book brings is simple but very serious. Its essential message is *the greatest need of the Church, and the thing which, above all others, believers ought to seek for with one mind and with their whole heart, is to be filled with the Spirit of God.*

In order to focalize our heart's attention to this message and to the blessing it contains, I have placed particular emphasis on certain main points:

1. It is the will of God that every believer should live entirely and unceasingly under the control of the Holy Spirit.

2. Apart from the fullness of the Spirit, it is utterly impossible that a believer or a church can ever live or work as God desires.

3. The lives and experiences of believers everywhere demonstrate that this blessing is in great neglect in the Church, and, alas! is seldom sought after.

4. This blessing is promised to us and prepared for us—God waits to give it to us. Because it is God's gift, our faith may expect it with the greatest confidence.

5. The great hindrance in receiving it is that the self-life and the world (which it uses for its own service and pleasure) seize the place that Christ ought to occupy.

6. We cannot be filled with the Spirit until we yield ourselves to be led by the Lord Jesus in the forsaking and sacrificing of everything that restricts His rule.

Despite the imperfection of my writings, I trust that this work will be a great blessing to believers. Let the reader be aware that because of the spiritual darkness which prevails in the Church, that, unless we take time to devote our heart and our thoughts to the real facts of the case, the promise of God will make no deep impression upon us. I hope through these chapters to demonstrate that God's blessing is in truth *the one thing needful,* and that to receive *this one thing*, we need to be prepared to sacrifice everything else we hold dear. I frankly invite believers to study this book carefully more than once. With the prevailing lack of the presence and operation of the Spirit in the Church, the spiritual truths concerning the need, and the fullness, and the reality of the Spirit's power obtaining mastery over us are deeply resisted. It is only through the exercise of self-sacrifice and keeping our minds occupied with these truths that we can ever obtain what might otherwise come to us at once.

Reflecting on what I have written, I feel there is one point on which I should have spoken more definitely. I refer to the role which persevering prayer must occupy in connection with this blessing. This book was not exclusively written for prayer at the season of Pentecost. *Every day ought to be a Pentecostal season in the Church of Christ.* By Pentecostal season let the reader understand that throughout the book I am referring to that original outpouring of the Holy Spirit on the disciples in the upper room which prevailed in the Church throughout the book of Acts. This season is meant to prevail throughout the year; and it seems to me now that I have insufficiently exhorted my readers to ceaseless calling upon God in the confidence that He will answer. Let me develop this thought.

When we read the book of Acts, we see that the filling with the Spirit and His mighty operation was always received through prayer. Recall, for example, what took place at Antioch. It was when the believers there were engaged in fasting and prayer that God regarded them as prepared to receive the revelation that they must separate Barnabas and Saul; and it was only after they had once more fasted and prayed that these two men departed, sent by the Holy Spirit (Acts 13:2, 3). They realized that the power and the direction needed *must come only from above.* Can our attitude be any different than theirs? I fear it is not so. We in like manner, even with fasting, must liberate ourselves as far as possible from the demands of the earthly life, even in that which otherwise appears quite lawful; our wholehearted commitment to God in prayer must not be less than that of the believers in Antioch. Let us never become weary or slack in prayer, but in union with other believers let us call upon Him day and night, entreating Him and even wearying Him by our incessant intercession, that the Holy Spirit may again take His rightful place and exercise full dominion in our lives and the Church as a whole. Intercession that He may again have His true place in the Church, be held in honor by all, and in everything reveal the glory of our Lord Jesus. To the believer who prays this in sincerity, God's answer will surely come.

True prayer is God's designed method to search and to cleanse the heart. Through it He questions the motives of my heart: Do I really desire what I pray for? Am I willing to cast out everything to make room for what God is prepared to give me? Is the prayer of my lips really the prayer of my life? Do I continue in intercession with God, waiting upon Him, in quiet trust, until He gives me this supernatural gift, *His own Spirit,* to be the spirit of my life every hour?

Our great need is to "pray always and not faint," setting ourselves before God with supplications and strong crying as His priests and the representatives of His Church. We are assured that He will hear us:

In my distress I called upon the Lord,
And cried unto my God:
He heard my voice out of his temple,
And my cry came before him, even into his ears.
He delivered me from my strong enemy . . .
He brought me forth also into a large place. (Ps. 18:6, 17,
19)

Believer, do you understand God's character? He desires to be trusted. He is oftentimes very near to us without our knowing it. He is a God who loves to reveal himself and His desires to us. Our place must be that of waiting on Him. "I had fainted, unless I had believed to see the goodness of the Lord in the land of the living. Wait on the Lord: be of good courage, and he shall strengthen thine heart: wait, I say, on the Lord" (Ps. 27:13, 14).

1

How It Is to Be Taught

"And it came to pass, that . . . Paul . . . came to Ephe- sus; and finding certain disciples, he said unto them, Have ye received the Holy Ghost since ye believed?" (Acts 19:1, 2).

It was nearly twenty years after the initial outpouring of the Holy Spirit that the incident which is referred to in Acts 19 took place. In the course of his third missionary journey, Paul came to Ephesus and found some disciples in whom he observed that there was something lacking in their belief or experience. Accordingly, he asked them: "Have ye received the Holy Ghost since ye believed?" Their reply was that they had never heard of the Holy Spirit. They had been baptized by disciples of John the Baptist, a baptism of repentance with a view to faith in Jesus as the One who was to come; concerning the great event of the outpouring of the Spirit or the significance of it, they

13

were still unacquainted. They came from a region of the country where the full Pentecostal preaching of the exalted Savior had not yet penetrated. Accordingly, Paul took them under his care and instructed them in the full gospel of the glorified Lord, who had received the Spirit from the Father and had sent Him down to this world, that every one of His believing disciples might also receive Him. Hearing this good news and believing it, they were baptized in the name of the Lord Jesus, who baptizes with the Holy Spirit. Paul then prayed for them and laid his hands upon them, and the Holy Spirit came upon them. In token of the fact that this whole transaction was a heavenly reality, they obtained a share in the Pentecostal miracle and spoke "with other tongues and prophesied" (19:6).

In these chapters it is my desire to bring to believers the message that there is a twofold Christian life. The one is that in which we experience something of the operations of the Holy Spirit, but do not yet receive Him as the Pentecostal Spirit, as the personal indwelling Guest, concerning whom we know that He has come to abide permanently in the heart. On the other hand, there is a more abundant life, in which the indwelling just referred to is known and the full joy and power of redemption are a fact of personal experience. It is essential that believers come to fully understand the distinction between these two conditions, and discern that the second of these is the express will of God concerning them, and therefore a possible experience for every believer. Only then will they humble themselves and confess the sinful and inconsistent elements that still mark their life; only then will we dare to hope that the Christian community will once more be restored to its Pentecostal power. With our eye fixed on this distinction, we desire to ponder the lessons presented to us in the record of this incident at Ephesus.

For a healthy Christian life, it is indispensable that we

know that we have received the Holy Spirit to dwell in us.

Had it been otherwise, Paul would never have asked the question: "Have ye received the Holy Ghost since ye believed?" These disciples were recognized as believing in Jesus as the One who was to come. This belief, however, was not enough. The disciples who walked with the Lord Jesus on earth were also true believers, yet He commanded them to not rest satisfied until they had received the Holy Spirit from himself in heaven. Paul, too, had seen the Lord in His heavenly glory and was by that vision led to conversion; yet even in his case the spiritual work he required to have done in him was not thereby completed. Ananias had to go to him and lay his hands upon him that he might receive the Holy Spirit. Only then could he become an effective witness for Christ. These facts teach us that there are two ways in which the Holy Spirit works in us. The first is the preparatory operation in which He simply acts on us but has not taken His dwelling place within us, though leading us to conversion and faith in Christ and ever urging us to all that is good and holy. The second is the higher and more advanced phase of His working when we receive Him as an abiding gift, as an indwelling Person, concerning whom we know that He assumes responsibility for our whole inner being, working in us both to will and to do. This is the ideal of the full Christian life.

There are disciples of Christ who know little or nothing of this conscious indwelling of the Holy Spirit.

It is of the utmost importance to comprehend this. The more we come under the conviction of its truth, the more completely we will understand the condition of the Church in our times and be enabled to discover where we ourselves really stand.

The condition I refer to becomes very plain when we consider what took place at Samaria. Philip the evangelist had preached there; many had been led to believe in Jesus and were baptized in His name; and there was great joy in that city. When the apostles heard this news, they sent Peter and John, who, when they came to Samaria, prayed that these new believers might receive the Holy Spirit (Acts 8:16, 17). This gift was thus something quite distinct from the working of the Spirit that led them to conversion and faith and joy in Jesus as Savior. It was something higher: for now from heaven, and by the glorified Lord himself, the Holy Spirit was imparted in power with His abiding indwelling to consecrate and fill their hearts.

Without this new experience, the Samaritan believers would still indeed have been Christians, but they would have remained weak, defective, and powerless; and thus it is that in our own days there are many believers that know nothing of this bestowment of the Holy Spirit. In the midst of much that is good and to be admired, often with much earnestness and zeal, the life of believers is still hampered by weakness and stumbling and disappointment. The reason for such weakness is often simply because they have never been brought into vitalizing contact with power from on high, because they have not received the Holy Spirit as the Pentecostal gift, to be possessed, and kept, and filled by Him.

It is the great work of the gospel ministry to lead believers to the Holy Spirit.

Wasn't it the great aim of the Lord Jesus, after He had personally educated and trained His disciples for three years, to lead them up to the point of waiting for the promise of the Father and receiving the Holy Spirit sent down from heaven? Wasn't this the chief object of Peter on the day of Pentecost, when, after charging those who were pricked in their hearts to repent and be baptized for the forgiveness of sins, he assured them that they should receive the Holy Spirit (Acts 2:38)? Wasn't this also what

Paul aimed at when in his Epistles he asked his fellow believers if they did not know that they were personally "a temple of the Holy Spirit" (1 Cor. 6:19), or reminded them that they had to be "filled with the Holy Spirit" (Eph. 5:18)? Yes: the supreme need of the believer's life is to receive the Holy Spirit, and when we have it, to be conscious of the fact and live in harmony with it. An evangelical minister cannot simply preach about the Holy Spirit from time to time or even oftentimes, but must direct all his efforts towards teaching his congregation that there can be no true worship except through the indwelling and unceasing operation of the Holy Spirit.

To lead believers to the Holy Spirit, the great lack in their life must be pointed out to them.

This was clearly Paul's intention: "Have ye received the Holy Ghost since ye believed?" Just as only those that are thirsty will drink water with eagerness and only those that are sick will desire a physician, so it is that only when believers are prepared to acknowledge the defective and sinful character of their spiritual condition will the preaching of the full blessing of Pentecost find an entrance into their hearts. As long as believers imagine that the only thing lacking in their life is more commitment, or more zeal, or more strength, and that if they only obtain these benefits they themselves will become all they ought to be, the preaching of a full salvation will be of little avail. It is only when they discover that they are not standing in a right relationship with the Holy Spirit, that they have only His initial workings, but do not yet know and honor Him in His indwelling, that the way to something higher will ever be open or even be desired. For this discovery, it is indispensable that the question should be put to every believer, as pointedly and as personally as possible: "Have ye received the Holy Ghost since ye believed?" When the answer comes forth as a deeply felt and utterly sincere no, the time of revival is not far off.

Believers must receive help to appropriate this blessing by faith.

In the Acts of the Apostles we often read about the laying on of hands and prayer. Even a man like Paul—whose conversion was a result of the direct revelation of Christ—had to receive the Spirit through the laying on of hands and prayer on the part of Ananias (Acts 9:17). This implies that there was to be among ministers of the gospel and believers generally a power of the Spirit which makes them the channel of faith and courage to others. Those who are weak must be helped to appropriate the blessing for themselves. But those who have and bring this blessing, as well as those who desire to have it, must realize and acknowledge their absolute dependence on the Lord and expect all from Him.

The gift of the Spirit is imparted only by God himself. Every fresh imparting of the Spirit comes from above. There must be frequent personal dealings with God. Both the minister whom God is to use for communicating the blessing of the Spirit as well as the believer who is to receive it must meet with God in immediate and personal intercourse. Every good gift comes from above: it is faith in this truth that will give us courage to expect with confidence and gladness that the full Pentecostal blessing is for us and that a life under the continual leading of the Holy Spirit is within our reach.

The proclamation and appropriation of this blessing will restore the Christian community to its original Pentecostal power.

On the day of Pentecost the speaking "with other tongues" and the prophesying was the result of being filled with the Spirit. Here at Ephesus, twenty years later, the very same miracle is again witnessed, as the visible token and pledge of the other glorious gifts of the Spirit. We should expect that where the reception of the Holy Spirit and the possibility of being filled with Him are proclaimed and received, the life of the believing community will be restored in all its Pentecostal power.

In our days there is an increasing acknowledgment of the lack of power in the Church. Despite the multiple improvements in Christian literature and education, there is neither the power of the divine salvation in believers, nor the power for conversion in preaching, nor the power in the conflict of the Church with worldliness and unbelief that, according to God's Word, we are to expect. The complaint is well justified. Would that the expression of it became so strong that the children of God, driven by an overwhelming sense of need, might cast themselves upon the great truth which the Word of God teaches—namely, that it is only when faith in the full Pentecostal blessing and the full enjoyment of it are found in the Christian Church that the members of it shall again find their strength and be able to accomplish the will of God.

The most urgent need of the Church is for men who are equipped to bear testimony to this blessing.

Whether it be of teachers like Peter and Paul, of deacons like Philip, or of ordinary believers like Ananias who came to Paul, this is our first need. It furnishes abundant reason why teachers and members of congregations should unitedly call upon God, that both in preaching and daily conversation there may be more manifest proof that those who declare Christ Jesus may declare Him as John the Baptist did, as the One who baptizes with the Holy Spirit. It is only those witnesses who stand forth as a personal testimony and living proof of the ministry of the Spirit whose word will have full entrance into the hearts of the people and exercise real influence over them. The first disciples received the baptism on their knees; on their knees they received it for others. It will be on our knees also that the full blessing will come to us today. On our knees: let this be the attitude in which we await the full blessing of our God, both in our individual and collective life.

Have you received the Holy Spirit since you believed? Let every reader submit himself to this heart-searching question. To be filled with the Holy Spirit of God, to have the full enjoyment of the Pentecostal blessing, is the will of God concerning us. Let us judge our life and our work before the Lord in the light of this question, and return the answer to God. Do not be afraid to confess before your Lord what is still lacking in you. Do not keep back, although you do not as yet fully understand what the blessing is or how it comes. The early disciples did not know that, yet they called upon the Lord and waited for it with prayer and supplications. Let your heart be filled with a deep conviction of what you lack, a desire for what God offers, a willingness to sacrifice everything for it, and you may rest assured that the marvel of Jerusalem and of Samaria, of Caesarea and Ephesus, will once again be repeated. We may, we shall, be filled with the Spirit. Amen.

2

How Glorious It Is

"They were all filled with the Holy Ghost. . . " (Acts 2:4).

Whenever we speak of being filled with the Holy Spirit, and desire to know exactly what it is, our thoughts always turn back to the day of Pentecost. There we see in God's light how glorious the blessing is that is brought from heaven by the Holy Spirit and with which He can fill the hearts of men.

What makes the great day of Pentecost doubly instructive for us is that we have learned to know very intimately the men who were then filled with the Spirit, by their training for three years with the Lord Jesus. Their failures, their character weaknesses, and their sins, all stand open to our view. But the blessing of Pentecost worked a complete transformation. They became entirely new men, so that one might truly say of them: "Old things are passed away; behold, all things are become new" (2 Cor. 5:17).

Close study of them and their example helps us in more than one way. It shows us that the Spirit will come to weak and sinful men. It teaches us how to be prepared for the blessing. It teaches us also—and this is the main point—how mighty and complete the revolution is that is brought to pass when the Holy Spirit is received in His fullness. Herein we see how glorious the grace is that awaits us if we press on to the full blessing of Pentecost.

The ever-abiding presence and indwelling of the Lord Jesus.

This is the first and principal blessing of the Pentecostal life. During the Lord's training of His disciples, He spared no pains in teaching and exhorting them, with the goal to renew and sanctify them. In most respects, however, they remained just what they were. The reason they did not change was that up to this point He was only the external Christ who stood outside of them and from without sought to work upon them by His word and His personal influence. With the advent of Pentecost this condition was entirely changed. In the Holy Spirit He came as the indwelling Christ, to become in the very innermost recesses of their being the life of their life. This is what He himself had promised: "I will not leave you comfortless: I *will come to you.* At that day ye shall know that I am in my Father, and ye in me, and I in you" (John 14:18, 20). This was the source of all the other blessings that came with Pentecost. Jesus Christ, the Crucified, the Glorified, the Lord from heaven, came in spiritual power by the Spirit, to impart to them that ever-abiding presence of their Lord that had been promised to them; and that in a way that was at once most intimate, all-powerful, and wholly divine: by the indwelling which truly makes Him their life. Jesus whom they had known in His earthly ministry, they now received by the Spirit in His heavenly glory within them. Instead of an outward Jesus near them, they now obtained the inward Jesus with them.

From this first and principal blessing sprang the second: *the Spirit of Jesus came into them as the life and the power of sanctification.*

At this beginning point I will note only one feature in this change. Remember how often the Lord rebuked His disciples for their pride and exhorted them to humility. Yet, they remained unchanged. Even on the night before His death, while gathered around the table of the Lord's Supper, there was a strife among them as to which of them should be the greatest (Luke 22:24). The outward teaching of the outward Christ, whatever other influences it may have exercised, was not sufficient to redeem them from the power of indwelling sin; this could only be achieved by the indwelling Christ. Only when Jesus descended into them by the Holy Spirit did they undergo a complete change. They received Him in His heavenly humility and subjection to the Father, and in His self-sacrifice for others, as their life. Henceforth all was changed. From then on they were animated by the spirit of the meek and lowly Jesus.

This, in very truth, is still the only way to real sanctification, to a life that actually overcomes sin. Many ministers and believers keep their minds occupied only with the external Christ on the Cross or in heaven, and wait for the blessing of His teaching and His working without understanding that the blessing of Pentecost brings Him *into us,* to work His life *in us.* Is it any wonder that they make so little progress in sanctification? Christ himself is of God made unto us sanctification (1 Cor. 1:30): and that in no other way than by our living and being moved and existing in Him, because He lives and abides in our heart and works all there.

An overflowing of the heart with the love of God is also

a part of the blessing of Pentecost.

Next to pride, lack of love—or, as we may put it in one word, lovelessness—was the second sin which the Lord repeatedly rebuked His disciples. These two sins have the same essential root: the self-seeking *I,* the desire for self-pleasing. The new commandment that He gave them, the token whereby all men should know that they were His disciples, was love to one another (John 13:34). How gloriously this was manifested on the day of Pentecost when the Spirit of the Lord shed abroad His love in the hearts of His own. The multitude of them that believed were as one heart, one soul: all things they possessed were held in common; no one said that anything that he had was his own (Acts 4:32). The kingdom of heaven with its life of love had come down to them. The spirit, the disposition, the wonderful love of Jesus, filled them, because He himself had come into them. All this remarkable change came with His presence.

How closely the mighty working of the Spirit and the indwelling of the Lord Jesus are bound up with a life in love appears from the prayer of Paul in behalf of the Ephesians, in which he asks that they might be strengthened with power *by the Spirit,* in order that *Christ might dwell in their hearts.* Then he makes this addition: "that ye, being rooted and grounded in love, may be able to comprehend with all the saints . . . the love of Christ, which passeth knowledge. . . " (Eph. 3:17–19). The filling with the Spirit and the indwelling of Christ bring of themselves a life that has its root, its joy, its power, its evidence in love, because the indwelling Christ himself is Love. Oh, how the love of God would fill the Church and convince the world that she has received a heavenliness into her life if the filling with the Spirit and the indwelling of Christ in the heart were recognized as the blessing which the Father has promised us!

The coming of the Spirit changed weakness and fear into courage and power.

Remember that it was the fear rising in his heart from the word of a woman that caused Peter to deny his Lord; remember, too, that same night all the disciples fled and forsook Him. Their hearts were affectionately attached to Him, and they were sincerely willing to do what they had promised and go to die with Him; but when it came to the crisis, they had neither courage nor power. They had to say: "To will is present with me, but how to perform I find not." After the blessing of the Spirit of Pentecost, there was no more question of merely willing apart from performing. By Christ dwelling in us God works both the willing and the doing. It was a transformed Peter who would on the day of Pentecost dare to confidently preach the Crucified One to thousands of hostile Jews. With amazing boldness he was able, in opposition to the leaders of the people, to say: "We ought to obey God rather than men" (Acts 5:29). With what courage and joy were Stephen and Paul and so many others enabled to encounter threatening and suffering and death: they did this triumphantly! It was because the Spirit of Christ, the Victor— yes, the glorified Christ himself—dwelt within them. It is the joy of the blessing of Pentecost that gives courage and power to speak for Jesus, because by it the whole heart is filled with Him.

The blessing of Pentecost makes the whole Word of God new.

How distinctly we see this fact in the case of the disciples. As with nearly all the Jews of that age, their ideas of the Messiah and the kingdom of God were utterly external and carnal. All the detailed instruction of the Lord Jesus throughout three long years did not detach their minds from these external thoughts. They were utterly unable to comprehend the doctrine of a suffering and dying

Messiah or the hope of His invisible spiritual dominion. Even after His resurrection He had to deal with their unbelieving spirit and their backwardness in understanding the Scriptures. With the coming of the day of Pentecost an entire change took place. The whole of their ancient Scriptures opened up before them. The light of the Holy Spirit in them illumined the Word. In the preaching of Peter and Stephen, in the addresses of Paul and James, we see how a divine light had shone upon the word of the Old Testament. They saw everything through the Spirit of this Jesus who had made His abode within them.

So it is meant to be with ourselves. We agree that it is absolutely essential that we should daily study the Scriptures and meditate upon them, and keep the word of God, alike in head and heart and daily walk. But let us constantly remember that it is only when we are filled with the Spirit that we can rightly and fully experience the spiritual power and truth of the Word. He is "the Spirit of truth." He alone guides into all truth when He dwells in us (John 16:13).

It is the blessing of Pentecost that gives power to bless others.

The divine power of the exalted Jesus to grant repentance and the forgiveness of sins is extended by Him through His servants whom He sends forth to proclaim these blessings. The minister or believer who desires to proclaim repentance and forgiveness through Jesus with success in winning souls must do the work in the power of the Spirit of this Jesus. The primary reason why so much evangelism is fruitless lies in the fact that these elements of truth are presented only as a doctrine, and that this attempt is made to secure a way to the hearts of the listeners in the mere power of human earnestness, reasoning, and eloquence. But little blessing is won by these means. It is the man that makes it his chief desire to be filled with the Spirit of God, and then by faith in the indwelling of Christ comes to be assured that the glorified Lord will speak and work in him, who will obtain blessing. It is true, indeed, that this blessing will not always be given in the very same measure or in the very same manner, but it will always certainly come when the believer allows the Lord to work in and through him. Both in proclamation and in the daily life of a believer, the full blessing of Pentecost is the sure way of becoming a blessing to others. "He that believeth on me," said Jesus, "out of his belly shall flow rivers of living water" (John 7:38). This He said of the Holy Spirit. A heart filled with the Spirit will overflow with the Spirit.

It is the blessing of Pentecost that will make the Church of Christ what God would have her be.

We have spoken of what the Spirit will do in individual believers. We should also consider what will happen when the Church as a whole apprehends her calling to be filled with the Spirit, and then exhibits the life and the power— yes, and the very presence—of her Lord to the world. We must not only seek and receive this blessing for ourselves, but we must remember that the full manifestation of what the blessing itself is cannot be given until the whole body of Christ is filled with it. "Whether one member suffer, all the members suffer with it. . . " (1 Cor. 12:26). If many members of the Church of Christ are content to remain without this blessing, the whole Church will suffer. Even in individual believers the blessing cannot come to its full manifestation. Therefore, it is of the utmost importance that we should not only think of what the being "filled with the Spirit" means for ourselves, but also consider what it will do for the Church, especially in our own neighborhood, and by her for all the world.

To this end, let us simply recall the morning of the day of Pentecost. At that point the Christian Church in Jerusalem consisted of only one hundred and twenty believers, most of them ordinary and uneducated fishermen, publicans, and humble women, an insignificant and despised gathering (Acts 1:15). Yet it was by these believers that the kingdom of God was to be proclaimed and extended: and they did it. By them, and those who were added to them, the power of Jewish prejudice and of pagan hardness of heart was overcome, and the Church of Christ won glorious triumphs. This grand result was achieved simply and only because the first Christian Church was filled with the Spirit. The members of it gave themselves wholly to the Lord. They allowed themselves to be filled and consecrated, governed and used only by Him. They yielded themselves to Him as instruments of His power. He dwelt in them and worked in them all His wondrous deeds.

It is to this same experience that the Church of Christ in our age must return. This is the only thing that will help her in the conflict with the darkness and power of sin and the world. She must be filled with the Spirit.

Beloved believers, this summons comes to you. "One thing is needful." Both for yourselves and the whole Church of the Lord, this is the one thing that is needful: we have to be filled with the Spirit. Do not imagine that you must comprehend or understand it all before you seek and find it. For those that wait upon Him God will do even that which has not yet entered into their heart to conceive. If you would taste the happiness, if you would know by personal experience the unutterable blessedness of having Jesus in the heart, of having in you His Spirit of holiness and humility, of love and self-sacrifice, of courage and power, as naturally and continuously as you have your own spirit; if you would have the Word of God in you as light and power and be enabled to carry it about as a blessing for others, if you would see the Church of Christ stand forth arrayed in her first splendor—then separate yourselves from everything that is evil, cast it utterly out of your heart, and fix your desire on this one thing: to be filled with the Spirit of God. Depend upon receiving this as your rightful heritage. Appropriate it and hold it fast by faith. It shall certainly be given to you.

3

How It Is Bestowed from Heaven

"If ye love me, keep my commandments. And I will pray the Father, and he shall give you another Comforter, that he may abide with you for ever; even the Spirit of truth. . ." (John 14:15–17).

A tree always lives according to the nature of the seed from which it sprang. Every living being is always guided and governed by the nature which it received at its birth. The same holds true in the Church of Christ. She received the promise and the law of her existence and her growth in that which was bestowed upon her in the Holy Spirit on the day of her birth. This is why it is so important for us to thoroughly understand the day of Pentecost and to not rest until we receive and experience what God did for His people on that day. Seeing how the blessing was first given from heaven and the attitude of heart that enabled the disciples to receive the Spirit, we shall have a scriptural precedent to know what remains to be done by ourselves to enjoy the same blessing. The first disciples serve us as biblical examples and forerunners on the way to the fullness of the Spirit.

What was it that enabled them to become the recipients of these heavenly gifts? What made them capable of receiving the unspeakable grace of the indwelling Three-One God? Understanding the answer to this question is the key to being filled with the Holy Spirit.

What do we find in these first disciples?

In the first place, there is the fact that *they were deeply attached to the Lord Jesus.*

The Son of God came into the world to enable man to partake of the divine life which He had with the Father. When He had completed the work in His own person by His obedience, and death, and resurrection, He was exalted to the throne of God on high in order that in spiritual power, in the might of the all-penetrating sovereign presence of God, His disciples and His Church might participate in His very own life. We read that the Holy Spirit "was not yet given; because that Jesus was not yet glorified" (John 7:39). It was only after His glorification that the Holy Spirit, as the Spirit of Godhead united with manhood, the Spirit of the complete indwelling of God in man, could be given. It is the Spirit of the glorified Jesus that the disciples received on the day of Pentecost, the Spirit of the Head, penetrating all the members of His body.

It is self-evident that if the fullness of the Spirit thus dwells in Jesus, *a personal relationship to Him is the first condition for the reception of the full gift of the Comforter.* It was towards this goal that the Lord Jesus throughout His three years' work on earth kept the disciples in such a close relationship with himself. He desired to attach them to himself. He wanted them to feel themselves truly one with Him. He wanted them to identify themselves with Him, as far as this was possible. By knowledge and fellowship, by love and obedience, they became inwardly knit to Him. This was their preparation for participating in the Spirit of His glorification.

The lesson taught here is extremely simple, but it is one of profound significance. There are many believers who trust in the Lord and are very zealous in His service, who eagerly desire to become holy, and yet who come short of this standard. It often seems that they cannot understand the promise of the Spirit. The thought of being filled with the Spirit exercises little influence upon them. The reason is obvious. There is lacking in their life that personal relationship to the Lord Jesus, that inward attachment to Him, that perfectly natural reference to Him as the best and nearest Friend, as the beloved Lord, which was so characteristic of the disciples. This, however, is absolutely indispensable. It is a heart that is entirely occupied with the Lord Jesus, and depends only upon Him, that can alone hope for the fullness of the Spirit.

They had left all for Jesus.

"Nothing for nothing." This proverb contains a deep truth. A thing that costs me nothing may nevertheless cost me much. It may bring me under an obligation to the giver and so cost me more than its worth. I may have so much trouble in receiving it and maintaining it that I may pay much more for it than the original price. "Nothing for nothing": the maxim holds good also in the life of the kingdom of heaven. The parables of the Pearl of great price and the Treasure hid in a field teach us that in order to obtain possession of the kingdom within us, we must sell all that we have. This is the very renunciation that Jesus literally demanded of the disciples who would follow Him. This is the requirement He so often repeated in His preaching: "He . . . that forsaketh not all that he hath, he cannot be my disciple" (Luke 14:33). The two worlds between which we stand are in such direct conflict with one another, and the world system in which we live exercises such a mighty influence over us, that it is often necessary for us, even by external and visible sacrifice, to withdraw from it. It was through their withdrawal from the world that Jesus trained His disciples to long for that which is heavenly. Only then could He prepare them to desire and receive the heavenly gift with an undivided heart.

The Lord did not leave us specific instructions as to how much of the world we are to abandon or in what manner. But by His Word He teaches us that without sacrifice, without a deliberate separation from the world and forsaking of it, we shall never make progress in our spiritual life. The spirit of this world has penetrated so deeply into us that we cannot comprehend it. We share in its desire for comfort and enjoyment, for self-pleasing and self-exaltation, without our knowing how impossible these things make it for us to be filled with the Spirit. Let us learn from the early disciples that to be filled from the heavenly world with the Spirit that dwells there, we must be entirely separate from the children of this world or from worldly believers. We must be ready and eager to live as entirely different men, who literally represent heaven upon earth, because we have received the Spirit of the King of Heaven.

They had despaired utterly of themselves and all that man can accomplish.

Man has two great enemies by whom the devil tempts him and with whom he has to contend. The one is the world without; the other is the self-life within. This last, the selfish *ego*, is much more dangerous and stronger than the first. It is quite possible for a man to have made much progress in forsaking the world while the self-life retains full dominion within him. This is graphically illustrated in the disciples. Peter could say with truth: "Lo! we have left all and followed thee." Yet how manifestly did the selfish *ego*, with its self-pleasing and its self-confidence, still retain its influence over him.

As the Lord at their first calling led them up to the point of forsaking their outward possessions and following Him, so shortly afterwards He began to teach them that a disciple must deny *himself* and lose his own life if he would be worthy of receiving His. He must hate not only father and mother, where this was necessary, but even his own life (Luke 14:26). It was love for this self-life, more than all love for family, that hindered Jesus from doing His work in the heart. It would cost them more to be redeemed from the selfish *ego* within them than to forsake the world around them. The self-life is the natural life of sinful man. The only liberation from it is by death—that is, by first dying to it and then living in the strength of the new life that comes from God.

The forsaking of the world began at the outset of the three years' discipleship. It was at the end of that period, at the Cross of Jesus, that dying to the self-life first took place. When they saw Him die, they learned to despair of themselves and of everything on which they had based their hope. Whether they thought of Him in contrast to the redemption which they had expected, or whether they thought of themselves and their shameful unfaithfulness towards Him, everything tended to fill them with despair. Little did they know that it was just this despair which was to prove the breaking up of their hard hearts—a death blow to the self-life and confidence in themselves. This brokenness enabled them to receive something entirely new—a divine life through the Spirit of the glorified Jesus in the innermost depths of their souls.

How we need to understand that there is nothing which so hampers us as a secret reliance on something in ourselves or in the Church around us which we imagine can help us! On the other hand, there is nothing that brings so much blessing as entirely despairing of ourselves and of all that is upon the earth, in the way of teaching us to turn our hearts only and wholly to heaven and to partake of the heavenly gift.

They received and held fast the promise of the Spirit given by the Lord Jesus.

In His farewell address on the night before His death, Jesus comforted His disciples in their sorrow over His departure with one great promise—the mission of the Holy Spirit (John 14–16). This was to be better than His own bodily presence among them. It would be to them the full fruit and power of His redemption. The divine Life—yes, He himself, with the Father—was to abide within them. The unheard-of wonder, the mystery of the ages, was to be their portion. They were to know that they were in Him and He in them. At His ascension from the Mount of Olives, this promise of the Spirit was the subject of the last words He addressed to them (Acts 1:8).

It is evident that the disciples still had little idea of what this promise signified. But however defective their understanding of it was, they held it fast; or rather, the promise held them fast and would not let them go. They all had only one thought: something has been promised to us by our Lord; it will give us a share in His heavenly power and glory; we know for certain that it is coming. Of what the thing itself was, or of what their experience of it was to be, they could give little account. It was enough for them that they had the word of the Lord. He would make it a reality within them.

It is this same disposition which we have so great a need of now. We also have the word of the Lord concerning the Spirit who is to descend from the throne in the power of His glorified life. "He that believeth in me, out of his heart shall flow rivers of living water." For us also it is the one thing needful to hold fast that word; to set our whole desire upon the fulfillment of it; to lay aside all else until we inherit the promise. The word from the mouth of Jesus concerning the reception of the Spirit in such measure that we shall be endued with power from on high must animate and fill us with strong desire, with firm and joyful assurance.

They waited upon the Father until the performance of the promise came and they were filled with the Spirit.

The ten days of waiting were for them days in which they "all continued with one accord in prayer and supplication" (Acts 1:14). It is not enough for us to endeavor to strengthen desire and to hold fast our confidence. The primary object is to set ourselves in close and abiding contact with God. The blessing must come from God; God himself must give it to us; we are to receive the gift directly from Him. What is promised us is a wonderful work of divine omnipotence and love. What we desire is the personal occupancy and indwelling of God the Holy Spirit. God himself must bestow this personally upon us. A man gives another a piece of bread or a sum of money. He gives it away and has nothing further to do with it. It is not thus with God's gift of the Holy Spirit. No: the Spirit is God. God is in the Spirit who comes to us, even as He was in the Son. The gift of the Spirit is the most personal act of the Godhead: it is the gift of himself unto us. We have to receive it in the very closest personal contact with God.

The clearer our insight into this principle, the more deeply we shall feel how little we can do to grasp the blessing by our own desiring, endeavoring, or believing. No: all our desiring, and striving, and believing can only result in a more complete acknowledgment that we ourselves can do nothing to receive it. It is the goodness of God alone that must give it; it is His omnipotence that must work it in us. Our disposition must be one of silent assurance that the Father desires to give it to us; that He will not keep us waiting one moment longer than is absolutely necessary; and that there shall not be a single soul which persists in waiting in the pathway of self-sacrifice and dependence that shall not be filled with the glory of God.

Every tree continues to grow from the root out of which it first sprang. The day of Pentecost was the planting of the Christian Church, and the Holy Spirit became the power of its life. Let us return to that experience. Our power is still there. We learn from the disciples what is really necessary. Attachment to Jesus, the abandonment of everything in the world for Him, despair of self and of all help from man, holding on to the Word of promise, and then waiting on God, "the living God"—this is the sure way of living in the joy and power of the Holy Spirit.

4

How It Is Enjoyed

"My speech and my preaching was not with enticing words of man's wisdom, but in demonstration of the Spirit and of power: that your faith should not stand in the wisdom of men, but in the power of God" (1 Cor. 2:4, 5).

Notice from this verse that Paul speaks of two kinds of preaching and two kinds of faith. The spirit of the preacher will have a great influence on the quality of the faith of the congregation. When the preaching of the Cross is given only in the words of human wisdom, the faith of the hearers will be in the wisdom of men. When the preaching is in demonstration of the Spirit and of power, the faith of the believers will be in the power of God, at once firm and strong. Preaching in the demonstration of the Spirit brings the double blessing of power in the word and power in the faith of those who receive that word. To determine the quality of a church's spiritual life, we must consider the preaching and the faith that springs from it. These criterion are sure indicators as to whether the full blessing of Pentecost is truly being manifested.

There are very few who are prepared to say that this is really the case. We hear complaints of believers' weaknesses and sin everywhere we go. Others who are not complaining should be—their silence is due to the prevalence of ignorance or self-satisfaction. We desire to concentrate our thoughts upon this fact until we come under the full conviction that the condition of the Church is marked by impotence, and that nothing can restore her but the return to a life in the full enjoyment of the blessing of Pentecost. The extent to which we know our deficiency will determine how much we desire and obtain restoration. Evaluating the Church in the light of what Jesus is willing and powerful to make her should awaken our hearts with longing for the way to receive the full life of the Spirit.

Think, for example, what little power over sin there is among believers.

The Spirit of Pentecost is the Holy Spirit, the Spirit of God's holiness. When He came upon the disciples in the upper room, how their lives were transformed! Their carnal thoughts were changed into spiritual insight, their pride into humility, their selfishness into love, their fear of man into courage and loyalty. Sin was cast out by the inflowing of the life of Jesus.

The life which the Lord has prepared for His people is a life of victory. It is not indeed victory to such an extent that there will be no temptations; nor will that victory destroy the strong natural desires that we call desires of the flesh (desires common to our humanity which if allowed to rule will produce the works of the flesh). But there is to be victory of such a kind that the indwelling power of the Spirit who fills us, the presence of the indwelling Savior, shall strengthen us against temptation and keep the natural desires of the flesh in subjection. A victory comparable to the light of day subduing the darkness of night.

Yet, to what extent do we see power for victory over sin in the Church of Christ? Even among earnest believers, we see much untruthfulness and lack of honor, pride and self-esteem, selfishness and lack of love. How faint are the traces of the image of Jesus—obedience, and humility, and love, and entire surrender to the will of God— seen even among the people of God. The truth is that we have become so accustomed to the confession of sin and unfaithfulness, of disobedience and backsliding, that it is no longer regarded as a matter for shame. We make the confession before each other, and then after the prayer rest comforted and content. Oh, brethren, let us rather feel humbled and mourn over it! It is because so little of the full blessing of the Spirit is enjoyed or sought for that believers still commit so much sin, and have therefore so much to confess. Let every sin, whether in ourselves or others, serve as a summons of a lacking of the Spirit of God among us. Let every instance of failure in the fear of the Lord, in love, and holiness, and entire surrender to the will of God only urge us the more unceasingly to call upon God to bring His Spirit once more to full dominion over the whole Church of Christ.

Think, too, how little there is of separation from the world.

When the Lord Jesus promised the Comforter, He said: "Whom the world cannot receive." The spirit of this world, which is devotion to the visible, is in irreconcilable antagonism with the Spirit of Jesus in heaven, where God and His will are everything. The world has rejected the Lord Jesus; and no matter how spiritual it may appear, the world at heart is still the same untamable foe. It was for this reason that Jesus said of His disciples, and as indicating one of their distinctive marks: "They are not of the world, even as I am not of the world" (John 17:16). This, too, is the reason why Paul said: "We have received, not the spirit of the world, but the Spirit which is of God. . ." (1 Cor. 2:12). The two spirits, the spirit of the world and the Spirit of God, are engaged in a life-and-death conflict with one another.

Therefore, God has always called on His people to separate themselves from the world, and to live as pilgrims whose treasure and whose heart are in heaven. But is this what we see among believers? Who would dare say so? When they attain a measure of unblamableness in walk and assurance of heaven, most believers consider that they are at liberty to enjoy the world as fully as others. There is little to be seen of true spirituality in conversation and walk, in character and commitment. Could the result be any different when the fullness of the Spirit is so little enjoyed and sought for? Nothing but light can drive out darkness; and nothing but the Spirit of heaven can expel the spirit of the world. Where a man does not surrender himself to be filled with the Spirit of Jesus and the Spirit of heaven, there can be no other result than that, Christian though he may be, he must remain under the power of the spirit of the world. Oh, listen to the piercing cry that rises from the whole Church of Christ: "Who shall rescue us from the power of this spirit of the world?" And let your answer be: "Nothing, no one, save the Spirit of God. I must be filled with the Spirit."

Think how little there is of steadfastness and growth in faith.

There is nothing which plagues ministers more than the many believers who for a time are full of zeal and then fall away. We see this not only among the young or in times of awakening, but even among many that have for years maintained a good confession. When they enter a new circle of influence or are tested by prosperity or any special form of temptation, they cease to persevere. What causes this to happen? Surely it is the result of preaching that is more with the wisdom of persuasive words than in demonstration of the Spirit and of power. Their faith stands in the wisdom and work of man rather than in the power of God. As long as they have the benefit of earnest and instructive preaching, they continue to stand; whenever they lose it, they begin to backslide. Because current preaching has so little in the demonstration of the Spirit, believers are failing to make vital contact with the living God.

For the same reason, much of the current faith among believers is not in the power of God. Even the Word of God—which should always only be a guide pointing *towards God himself*—becomes all too frequently a veil with the study of which the soul becomes occupied, and is thus kept back from meeting with God. The Word, the preaching, and even the minister of grace become a hindrance instead of a help if they are not in demonstration of the Spirit. All external means of grace are things that inevitably change and fade. It is the Spirit alone that works a faith which stands in the power of God, and so remains strong and unwavering.

Why is it that there are so many who do not continue to stand? Let God's answer penetrate deeply into our hearts. It is the result of our failure to be a demonstration of the Spirit. Let every sad discovery of congregations, or of smaller groups, or of individuals that do not remain steadfast, or that do not grow in grace, serve as a summons to us that the full blessing of Pentecost is lost. This is what we long for and must have from God. Let all that is within us begin to thirst and cry out: "Come from the four winds, O thou Spirit of God, and breathe upon these dead souls, that they may live."

*Think how little there is of power for service towards
the lost.*

What an immense army of workers there is in Christian countries. How varied and unceasing is the preaching
of the Word. Sunday school teachers are to be numbered
by hundreds of thousands. How great is the number of
Christian parents that teach their children the Word of
God and desire to bring them to the Lord as Savior. Yet
how widespread is the acknowledgment of the little fruit
that springs from all this work. How many there are who,
notwithstanding all they hear and in spite of the fact that
they are by no means indifferent, are yet never touched
by God's power and helped to make a definite choice of
salvation. How many also there are who from youth to old
age are well-grounded with the Word of God but are never
seized by it in the depths of their heart. They find it good,
and pleasing, and instructive to attend church, but they
have never felt the power of the Word as a hammer, and
a sword, and a fire. The reason they are so little disturbed
is that the preaching they listen to is so little in demonstration of the Spirit and of power. Alas! how much evidence does it take to convince us that there is a great lack
of the full blessing of Pentecost.

Does the blame for this go to ministers or to congregations? My belief is that it belongs to both. The ministers
are the offspring of the Christian community. Ministers
are very dependent on the life that is in their congregations. When a congregation finds satisfaction in the merely
acceptable and instructive preaching of a young minister,
it encourages him to go forward on the same path, while
he should rather be helped by its elder or more advanced
believers to earnestly seek the demonstration of the Spirit.
When a minister does not lead his congregation (either in
public worship or in private prayer) to really expect everything from the Spirit of God, then he is tempted, both for
himself and his people, to put confidence in the wisdom of

man and the work of man. Oh, that we could lay it to heart, that, in the midst of all our lamentation over increasing worldliness and widespread indifference, the great cause is the lack of the full blessing of Pentecost among ourselves! This alone gives power from on high which can break down and touch the hard hearts of men.

Think how little preparedness there is for self-sacrifice in behalf of the extension of the kingdom of God.

When the Lord Jesus at His ascension promised the Holy Spirit, it was as a power in us to work for Him. "Ye shall receive power, after that the Holy Ghost is come upon you: and ye shall be my witnesses unto me . . . unto the uttermost part of the earth" (Acts 1:8). The goal of Pentecost was simply to complete the equipment of His servants for His work as King upon the earth. No sooner did the Spirit descend upon them than they began to witness for Him. The Spirit filled them with the desire and the impulse, with the courage and the power, to brave all hostility and danger, to endure all suffering and persecution, if only they could succeed in making Jesus known as Lord. The Spirit of Pentecost was that true missionary Spirit which seeks to win the whole world for Jesus Christ.

It has been said recently that the missionary spirit is so much on the increase. Yet when congregations and individuals reflect carefully on how little effort is given toward the missionary enterprise in comparison with what is given to their own interests, we see at once how feebly this question is still kindled in our hearts: "What more can I still sacrifice for Jesus? He offered himself for me. I will offer myself wholly for Him and His work." It has been well said that the Lord measures our gifts not according to what we give, but according to what we retain. He who stands beside the treasury and observes what is cast into it still finds a few who, like the widow, cast in all their living. But, alas! how many there are who have given only what they could never miss and what costs them little or no sacrifice. How different it would be if the full blessing of Pentecost began to flow in. How the hearts of men would burn with love to Jesus, and out of very joy be impelled to give everything that He might be known as the Savior throughout the world and that all might know His love.

Stop and consider the condition of the Church on earth, of the Christian community around you, of your own heart. Is there the cry: "The full blessing of Pentecost: how little is it known"? Ponder the present lack of sanctification, of separation from the world, of steadfastness among professing believers, of conversions among the unsaved, and of self-sacrifice for the kingdom of God, and let the sad reality deepen in your soul the conviction that the Church is at present suffering from one great evil—the lack of the blessing of Pentecost. There will be neither healing nor restoration from her fall, and no renewing of her power, except by her being filled with the Spirit of God.

Let us then never cease to speak, think, mourn, and pray over this trouble until this "one thing needful" becomes the one thing that occupies our hearts. Restoration is not easy. It will perhaps not come all at once: it may be a slow process. The disciples of Jesus required every day with Jesus for three long years to prepare them for it. We should not be unduly discouraged if the transformation we long for does not take place immediately. Let us feel the need and lay it to heart. Let us continue steadfastly in prayer. Let us stand fast in faith. The blessing of Pentecost is the birthright of the Church, the pledge of our inheritance, something that belongs to us here on earth. Faith can never be put to shame. Cleaving to Jesus with purpose of heart can never be in vain. The hour will surely come when, if we believe perseveringly in Him, out of our hearts too will flow rivers of living water. Amen.

5

How the Blessing Is Hindered

"Then said Jesus unto his disciples, If any man will come after me, let him deny himself, and take up his cross, and follow me. For whosoever will save his life shall lose it: and whosoever shall lose his life for my sake shall find it" (Matt. 16:24, 25).

Many sincerely seek the full blessing of Pentecost and yet do not find it. The question comes as to what causes this failure. The answer is multiple—every person is different. Sometimes the answer points in the direction of one or another sin which is still permitted. Worldliness, lovelessness, lack of humility, ignorance of the secret of walking in the way of faith—these, and indeed many more causes, could be mentioned with justice. There are, however, many who think they have come to the Lord with the source of failure that still remains in them, and have sincerely confessed it and put it away, and yet complain

46

that the blessing does not come. For them it is particularly necessary to point out that there still remains one great hindrance—the root from which all other hindrances have their beginning. This root is nothing other than our individual self, the hidden life of self with its varied forms of self-seeking, self-pleasing, self-confidence, and self-satisfaction. The more one strives to receive the blessing and desires to know what prevents him, the more certainly he will be led to the discovery that it is here the great evil lies. He himself is his worst foe: he must be liberated from himself; the self-life to which he clings must be utterly lost. Only then can the life of God entirely fill him.

This is taught in the words of the Lord Jesus to Peter. Peter had uttered such a glorious confession of his Lord that Jesus said to him: "Blessed art thou, Simon Bar-Jona: for flesh and blood hath not revealed it unto thee, but my Father which is in heaven." But when the Lord began to speak of His death by crucifixion, the selfsame Peter was seduced by Satan to say: "Be it far from thee, Lord: this shall not be unto thee" (Matt. 16:17, 22). The Lord then said that not only must He himself lay down His life, but that this same sacrifice was to be made by every disciple. Every disciple must deny himself and take up his cross in order that he himself may be crucified and put to death on it. He that desires to save his life will lose it; and he that is prepared to lose his life for Christ's sake will find it.

You see, then, what the Lord teaches and requires. Peter had learned through the Father to know Christ as the Son of God, but he did not yet know Him as the Crucified One. Of the absolute necessity of the Cross, and death on the Cross, he as yet knew nothing. It may be the same with a believer today. He knows the Lord Jesus as Savior; he desires to know him better, yes, fully; but he does not yet understand that it is necessary that he must have a deeper discernment of the death of the Cross as a death which he himself must die; that he must actually deny, and hate, and lose his life—his whole life and being in the world—before he can receive the full life of God.

This is a difficult requirement. And why is this so? Why should a Christian be called upon to always deny himself, his own feelings, and will, and pleasure? Why must he part with his life—that life which to maintain a man is prepared to make any sacrifice? Why should a man hate and lose his life? The answer is very simple. It is because that life is so completely under the power of sin and death that it has to be utterly denied and sacrificed. The self-life must be wholly taken away to make room for the life of God. He that would have the full, the overflowing life of God, must utterly deny and lose his own life.

Do you see it now? There is only one great hindrance to the full blessing of Pentecost. It lies in the fact that two diverse things cannot at one and the same time occupy the very same place. Your own life and the life of God cannot fill the heart at the same time. Your life hinders the entrance of the life of God. When your own life is cast out, the life of God will fill you. So long as *I myself* am still something, *Jesus himself* cannot be everything. Self-life must be expelled; then the Spirit of Jesus will flow in. Let every seeker of the full blessing of Pentecost accept this principle and hold it fast. The subject is of such importance that I want to make it still clearer by pointing out the chief lessons which these words of the Lord Jesus teach us.

Our life, our individual self, is entirely and completely under the power of sin.

When God created the angels and man, He gave them a separate personality, a power over themselves, with the intention that they should of their own free will present and offer up that life, that individual self, to Him—that He in turn might fill them with His life and His glory.

This was to be the highest blessedness of the creature. It was to be a vessel filled with the life and the perfection of God. The fall of both angels and of men consisted of nothing but the perversion of their life, their will, their personality, away from God, in order to please *themselves.* This self-exaltation was the pride that changed the angels into demons and cast them out of heaven. This pride was the infernal poison that the serpent breathed into the ear and the heart of Eve. Man turned himself away from God to find delight in himself and the world. His life, his whole individuality, was perverted and withdrawn from the control of God that he might seek and serve *himself.* It was no wonder that Jesus was saying they must hate, must utterly lose *that life,* before the full life of the Spirit of God could be theirs. To the minutest details, always and in everything, they must deny that self-life; otherwise the life of God could not possibly fill them. He that "will come after me, let him deny *himself,* and take up his cross, and follow me" (Matt. 16:24).

This deep conviction of sin's corruption of our personality, manifesting itself in the fact that even the Christian still pleases himself in many things, is still lacking in many people. It appears to them both strange and harsh when we say that the believer is never free to follow his own feelings, that self-denial is a requirement that must prevail in every sphere of life and without any exceptions. The Lord has never withdrawn His words: "He that forsaketh not all that he hath, he cannot be my disciple" (Luke 14:33). Let the believer take these words to heart.

Our own life must be utterly cast aside to make full room for the life of God.

At the time of his conversion the new believer has little understanding of this requirement. He receives the seed of the new life into his heart while the natural life is still strong. This was Peter's condition when the Lord addressed to him the words that have been quoted. He was a disciple, but alas! how defective and incomplete. When his Lord was to die, instead of denying himself, he denied his Lord. But that grievous failure brought him at last to that despair of himself which caused him to go out and weep bitterly, and so prepared him for losing entirely his own life and for being wholly filled with the life of Jesus.

This is the point to which we must all come. As long as the believer imagines that in some things—for example, in his eating and drinking, in the spending of his time or money, in his thinking and speaking about others—he still has the right and the liberty to follow his own wishes, to please himself, to maintain his own life, he cannot possibly receive the full blessing of Pentecost.

My brethren, it is an unspeakably holy and glorious thing that a man can be filled with the Spirit of God. It demands inevitably that the present occupant and governor of the heart, our individual self, shall himself be cast down, and that everything within it, everything wholly and entirely, shall be surrendered into the hands of the Spirit of God. Would that we could understand that the joy and power of being filled with the Spirit will come when we comply with the first and principal condition—that He alone shall be acknowledged as our Life and our Leader.

It is absolutely impossible for the believer to bring about this great transformation.

At no stage of our spiritual career are the power and the deceitfulness of our individual self and the self-life more manifest than in the attempt to grasp the full blessing of Pentecost. Many try to appropriate this blessing, and that by a great variety of efforts. They do not succeed, and they are not able to discover the reason why. They forget that self-will can never cast out self-will: that self can never mortify itself. Happy is the man who is brought to the point of acknowledging his helplessness and impotence. Here he must cease to expect anything from his own life and strength, but rather will lay himself down in the presence of the Lord as one who is impotent and dead, that he may really receive the blessing from Him.

It was not Peter that prepared himself for the day of Pentecost or brought down the Pentecostal blessing from heaven; it was his Lord that did all this for him. His part was to despair of himself and yield himself to his Lord to accomplish in him what He had promised. This also is your part, believer, while yielding obedience to this call, to deny *yourself,* and to lose *your own life,* and in the presence of the Lord to sink down in your nothingness and impotence. Set your heart before Him in deep humility, and silent patience, and childlike submission. The humility that is prepared to be nothing, the patience that will wait for Him and His time, the submission that will yield itself wholly that He may do what He desires is all that you can do. Jesus summons you to follow Him. Remember how He first sacrificed His will, and when He laid down His life into the hands of the Father, and went down into the grave, waited till God raised Him again to life. Be ready to lay down your life in weakness, and be assured that God will raise it up again in power with the fullness of the Spirit. Be done with the strength of personal efforts; abandon the dominion of your own power of apprehension. "Not by might, nor by power, but by my Spirit, saith the Lord" (Zech. 4:6).

It is the surrender of faith to Jesus in His self-humiliation and death that opens the way to the full blessing of Pentecost.

But, you say: "Who can do all this? Who can sacrifice everything and die and lay down his life utterly as Jesus did? To man such a surrender is impossible." I agree. But *"with God* all things are possible." You cannot literally follow Jesus, and like Him go down into death and the grave. That ever remains beyond your power. Never will our individual self yield itself up to death or rest quietly in the grave. But listen to the good news. In Christ you have died and have been buried. The power of His dying, of His willing surrender of His spirit into the hands of the Father, of His silent resting in the grave, *works in you*. In faith in this working, however little you may understand it—in faith in this working in you of the spirit and the power of the death and the life of the Lord Jesus, yield yourself willingly to lose your life.

Towards this goal, begin to regard the denying of yourself as the first and most necessary work of every day. Remember that the great hindrance in the way of the life of Pentecost is the self-life. Believe in the sinfulness, the detestableness, of that life: not on account of its gross external sins, but because it sets itself in the place of God; seeks, and pleases, and honors itself more than God. Exercise yourself in what Jesus lays upon you, and hate your own life as your own worst foe and as the foe of God. Begin to see what the full blessing is that Jesus has prepared for you and which He bestowed at Pentecost—namely, His own life, His own indwelling; and count nothing too precious or too costly to give as an exchange for this pearl of great price.

Are you sincere about being filled with the Spirit of God? Is it your great desire to know what hinders you from obtaining it? Take the word of our Lord and keep it in your heart. Take it and go with it to himself. *He is able to make you understand, and consider, and experience it. It is He who baptizes with the Holy Spirit.* Let everything in you that belongs to self be sacrificed to Him, and be counted as loss, and cast away to give place to himself. He who by His death obtained the Spirit, who prepared Peter for Pentecost in the fellowship of His suffering, has your guidance in His hands. Trust, oh, trust Him, your own Jesus. He baptizes with the Spirit, beyond doubt or question: deny yourself and follow Him; lose your own life and find His. Let Him impart himself in the place you have retained for yourself. From him there will flow rivers of living waters. Amen.

6

How It Is Received by Us

"Be not drunk with wine, wherein is excess, but be filled with the Spirit" (Eph. 5:18).

The command to be filled with the Spirit is just as imperative as the command to not be drunk with wine. As clearly as we are not to be guilty of the vice are we bound to obedience to the positive injunction. The same God who calls upon us to live in sobriety urges us with equal earnestness to be filled with the Spirit. His command is the sure guarantee that He himself will give what He desires us to possess. With full confidence in this fact, let us ask in all simplicity for insight into the way that we should live in the will of God, as those who would be filled with the Spirit. I would like to suggest to those who sincerely seek for this blessing some directions for receiving it.

The full blessing of Pentecost is the inheritance of all the children of God.

This is the first principle we have to enunciate. There are many believers who do not believe this. They think that the day of Pentecost was only the birthday feast of the Church, and that it was thus a time of blessing and of power which was not destined to endure. The command to be filled with the Spirit is of little significance to them. The result is that they never sincerely seek to receive the full blessing. They sit back and are content with the weak and defective life in which the Church of the day exists.

Is this the case with you? Far be it from us. In order to carry on her work in the world, the Church requires the full blessing. To please the Lord and to live a life of holiness and joy and power, you too have need of it. To manifest His presence, and indwelling, and glory in you, Jesus commands that you be filled with the Spirit. Come to terms with the full blessing of Pentecost as a sacred reality. A child of God may and must have it. Take time to contemplate it and allow yourself to be fully possessed by the thought of its glorious significance and power. A firm confidence that the blessing is actually within our reach is the first step towards obtaining it and a powerful impulse in the pursuit.

I do not as yet have this blessing.

This is the second step towards it. You may ask why it should be necessary to believe this. Let me briefly state the reasons why I consider it of importance.

The first is that there are many believers who think they already have the Holy Spirit, and that all they need is to be more faithful in their commitment to know and to obey Him. They think they are already standing in God's grace, and that they only need to make better use of the life they possess. They imagine that they have all that is necessary for continued growth. On the contrary, it is my deep conviction that they are in a deceived state and have need of a healing as divine and effective as that which the blind and lame received from Jesus' ministry. Just as the first condition of my recovery from a physical illness is the knowledge that I am sick, so it is absolutely necessary for them to discover and acknowledge that they do not live the life of Pentecost, that they do not walk in the fullness and the joy of the Spirit.

Once this first conviction is thoroughly clear to them, they will be prepared for another consideration—they need to acknowledge the guiltiness of their condition. They need to see that if they have not yet obeyed the command to "be filled with the Spirit," this defect is to be ascribed to sluggishness, and self-satisfaction and unbelief. This conviction should be acknowledged with the shame that they have despised what God had prepared for them. When the confession that they have not yet received the full blessing is deeply rooted in them, there will spring from it a stronger impulse to attain to it. Take, then, this thought and let it work in you with power: "No: it is true that I do not as yet have the full blessing."

The thought that will come next in succession is: *This blessing is for me.*

I have spoken of those who suppose that the full blessing of Pentecost was only for the first Christian community. There are others who acknowledge that it was intended also for the Church of later times but still think that all are not entitled to expect it. Eminent believers, the leaders of the Church, and such as have time and abundant opportunity to occupy their minds with such attainments may well cherish the hope of receiving this blessing, but it is not to be expected by ordinary members of the churches. Any one of these might reasonably say: "My unfavorable circumstances, my unfortunate disposition, my lack of ability, and similar difficulties, make it impossible for me to realize this ideal. God will not expect this of me: He has not destined me to obtain it."

Do not be deceived by such shallow views. All the members of a body, even to the very least, must be healthy before the body as a whole can be healthy. The indwelling, the fullness of the Spirit, is nothing but the entire healthfulness of the body of Christ. Be assured that the blessing is for you. In your own little measure you can at least be full. In this respect the Father makes no exceptions. A great distinction prevails in the matter of gifts, and calling, and circumstances; but there can be no distinction in the love of the Father and His desire to see every one of His children in full health and in the full enjoyment of the Spirit of adoption. Learn, then, to express and to repeat over again the conviction: *"This blessing is for me.* My Father desires that He may fill me with His Spirit. The blessing lies before me, to be taken with my full consent. I will no longer despise by unbelief what falls to me as my birthright. With my whole heart I will say: 'This blessing is for me.' "

I cannot grasp this blessing in my own power.

Whenever a believer begins to strive for this blessing, he generally makes a variety of efforts to reach after the faith, and obedience, and humility, and submission which are the conditions of obtaining it. Then, when he does not succeed, he is tempted to blame himself, and if he does not become utterly discouraged, he rouses himself to still stronger effort and greater zeal. All this struggling is not without its value and its use. It has its use, however, in ways other than they had anticipated. It does the very work that the law does—that is to say, it brings us to the knowledge of our entire impotence; it leads us to that despair of ourselves in which we become willing to give God the place that belongs to Him. This lesson is entirely indispensable. "I can neither bestow this blessing on myself nor take it. It is God alone that must work it in me."

The blessing of Pentecost is a supernatural gift, a wonderful act of God in the soul. The life of God in every soul is just as truly a work of God as when that life was first manifested in Jesus Christ. A believer can do as little to bring the full life of the Spirit to function in his soul as the Virgin Mary did to conceive her supernatural child (Luke 1:38). He can only receive it as the gift of God. The impartation of this heavenly blessing is as entirely an act of God as the resurrection of Christ from the dead was His divine work. As Christ Jesus had wholly and entirely to go down unto death, and utterly lay aside the life He had, in order to receive a new life from God, so must the believer abandon all power and hope of his own to receive this full blessing as a free gift of divine omnipotence. This acknowledgment of our utter impotence, this descent into true self-despair, is indispensable if we would enjoy this supreme blessing.

I must have this blessing at any cost.

To get possession of the pearl of great price, the merchant man sold *all that he had*. The full blessing of Pentecost is to be obtained at no smaller price. He that would have it must sell all, must forsake all: sin to its smallest item, the love of the world in its most innocent forms, self-will in its simplest and most natural expressions, every faculty of our personality, every moment of our life, every pleasure that feeds our self-complacency, every exercise of our body, soul, and spirit—all must be surrendered to the power of the Spirit of God. In nothing can independent control or independent force have a place: *everything* must be under the leading of the Spirit. One must say: "Cost what it may, I am determined to have this blessing." Only the vessel that is utterly empty of everything can be filled and overflow with this living water.

We know that there is often a great gulf between the

will and the deed. Even when God has worked the willing, the doing does not always come at once. But it will come wherever a man surrenders himself to the will which God has worked, and openly expresses his consent in the presence of God. This, accordingly, is what must be done by the believer who intends to be sincerely ready to part with everything, even though he feels that he has no power to accomplish it. The selling price is not always paid at the moment; nevertheless, the purchaser may become the possessor as soon as the sale is concluded and security is given for the payment. May this be your declaration today: "Cost what it may, I will have this blessing." Jesus is surety that you will have power to abandon everything. Express your decision in the presence of God with confidence and perseverance. Repeat it before your own conscience and say: "I am a purchaser of the Pearl of great price: I have offered everything to obtain the full blessing of Pentecost. I have said to God that I must, I will have it. By this decision I abide. I must, I will have it."

In faith that God accepts my surrender and gives this blessing as a gift, I appropriate it for myself.

There is a great difference between the appropriation of a blessing by faith and the actual experience of it. Because believers fail to understand this they often become discouraged when they do not immediately experience the feeling and the enjoyment of what is promised them. From the moment that you have chosen to forsake all and count it but loss for the full blessing of Pentecost, your part is to believe that He receives your offer and that He bestows upon you the fullness of the Spirit. Yet you say at that time you did not notice any marked change in your experience. It is as if everything in you remained in its old condition. Now, however, is just the very time to persevere in faith. Learn by faith to be as sure as if you had seen it written in heaven that God has accepted your surrender of everything as a certain and completed transaction. In this faith look upon yourself as a man who is known to God as one that has sold everything to obtain this heavenly treasure. Believe that God has bestowed upon you the fullness of the Spirit. In this faith regard yourself as on the way to knowing the full blessing also in feeling and experience. Believe that God will order this blessing to break forth and be revealed in you. In this faith let your life be a life of joyful thanksgiving and expectation. God will not disappoint you.

Now I count upon God and wait upon Him to reveal within me the blessing which He has bestowed upon me.

Faith must lead me to the actual inheritance of the promise, to the experience and enjoyment of it. Do not rest content with a belief that does not lead to experience. Rest in God by faith in the full assurance that He can make himself known to you in a manner that is truly divine. At times the whole process may appear to you too great and too wonderful, and really impossible. Be not afraid. The more clearly you discern the amazing elements in the fact that you have said to the Eternal Holy God that He may have you to make you full of His Holy Spirit here on earth, the more you will feel what a miracle of the grace of God it must be. There may be things in you that you are not aware of, which hinder the breaking forth of the blessing. God is committed to putting them aside. Let them be consumed in the fire of strong burning desire. Let them be annihilated in the flame of God's countenance and His love. Let your expectation be fixed upon the Lord your God. He who in a frail woman revealed the divine life in the infant Jesus, He that raised up the dead Jesus to the life of glory, He can—He will, indeed—just as miraculously bring this heavenly blessing to fruition in you, so that you may be filled with the Holy Spirit and that you may know, not by reasoning but by experience, that you have actually received the Holy Spirit.

Dear believer, I entreat you to this summons. God promises, God desires to make you full of the Holy Spirit. He desires that your whole personality and life be under the power of the Holy Spirit. He asks if you on your part are willing, if you really desire to have it. Let there be in your answer no uncertain sound, but let all that is within you cry out: "Yes, Lord, with all my heart." Let this promise of God become the chief element in your life, the most precious, the chief, the only thing you seek. Do not be content to think and pray over it, but this very day enter into a transaction with God that will permit no doubts concerning the choice you have made.

When you have made this choice, hold firmly to the chief element in it—the faith that expects this blessing as a miracle of divine omnipotence. The more earnestly you exercise that faith, the more it will teach you that your heart must be entirely emptied and set free from every fetter, to be filled with the Spirit, to be occupied by the indwelling Christ. Consider yourself in faith as a man fully surrendered to God and as a man who must receive the full blessing. You may take it for granted that it will surely come. Amen.

7

How It May Be Kept

"But ye . . . praying in the Holy Ghost, keep yourselves in the love of God. . . . Now unto him that is able to keep you from falling . . . to the only wise God our Savior, be glory . . . both now and ever. Amen" (Jude 20, 21, 24, 25).

Is it possible for someone who has the full blessing of Pentecost to lose it? Yes: undoubtedly. God does not bestow this gift with such constraint that a man retains it whether he desires it or not. No: this blessing is entrusted to him as a talent which must be used; and only by use does it become secure and win success. Just as the Lord Jesus after He was baptized with the Holy Spirit had to be perfected by obedience and submission to the leading of the Spirit, so the believer who has received the blessing of Pentecost has to see that he guards safely the deposit that has been entrusted to him.

Scripture points us to the fact that our keeping the

blessing consists in our entrusting it to the Lord to be kept by Him. Paul places these two ideas alongside one another in his second letter to Timothy: "He is able to keep that which I have committed unto him"; "That good thing which was committed unto thee, keep by the Holy Ghost which dwelleth in us" (1:12, 14). Jude also, after saying, "Keep yourselves in the love of God," adds the doxology: "Unto him that is able to keep you . . . be glory." The secret of preserving the blessing is the exercise of a humble dependence on the Lord who keeps us and on the Spirit by whom we ourselves are kept in close fellowship with Him. It is with this blessing as with the manna that fell in the wilderness: it must be renewed from heaven daily. It is with the new heavenly life as with the life we live on earth: the fresh air that sustains it must be drawn in every moment from without and from above. Let us see how this sustained life takes place.

Jesus, who gave us the blessing, will maintain it for us.
Jesus is the Keeper of Israel. This is His name and this is His work. God not only created the world but also keeps and upholds it. Jesus is not content with simply giving the blessing of Pentecost: He will also maintain it every moment. The Holy Spirit is not a power that in any sense is subordinate to us, that is given to us for our personal use; He is a power that is over and above us, that possesses and energizes us, a power by which Jesus in heaven will carry forward His work from moment to moment. Our proper place and attitude must always be that of the deepest dependence, a sinking down in our own nothingness and impotence. Our chief concern is to let Jesus do His work within us.

As long as a believer does not discern this truth there will always be in it a certain dread of receiving the full blessing. He will be inclined to say: "I will not be able to continue in that holy life. Such a life may be experienced from time to time, but never maintained." These thoughts only show what a feeble grasp such a one has of the great reality. When Jesus comes by the Spirit to dwell in my heart and to live in me, He will actually work out the maintenance of the blessing and regard my whole inner life as His special care. He who believes this truth sees that the life in the blessing of Pentecost, while it can never be relieved of the necessity of watchfulness, is a life that is freed from anxiety and ought to be characterized by continued gladness. The Lord has come into His holy temple. There He will abide and work out everything. He desires only this one thing—that the soul shall know and honor Him as its faithful Shepherd, its Almighty Keeper. Jesus, who gives the blessing of Pentecost, will certainly maintain it in us.

Jesus will maintain the blessing, as He gave it, by faith.
The law that prevails at every stage in the progress of the kingdom of God is: "Be it unto you according to your faith." The faith that in the first reception of the Lord Jesus was as small as a grain of mustard seed must, in the course of the Christian life, always grow in order that it shall see more and receive and enjoy more of the fullness that is in the Lord. Paul wrote to the Galatians: "I live; yet not I, but Christ liveth in me: and the life which I now live in the flesh I live by faith" (2:20). His faith was as broad and boundless and unceasing as were the needs of his life and work. In everything and at all times, without ceasing, he trusted in Jesus to do all. His faith was wide and abundant—like the glorious energy that flows from Jesus for the enrichment of His people. He had surrendered his whole life to Jesus: he himself lived no longer. By a continuous and unrestricted faith he gave Jesus the liberty of energizing his life without ceasing and without limitation.

The fullness of the Spirit is not a gift that is bestowed

once for all as a part of the heavenly life. No: it is not so. It is rather a constantly flowing stream of the river of the water of life that issues from beneath the throne of God and of the Lamb. It is an uninterrupted communication of the life and the love of Jesus, the most personal and intimate association of the Lord with His own upon the earth. It is by the faith which discerns this truth, and assents to it, and holds to it with joy, that Jesus will certainly do His work of keeping.

Jesus maintains this blessing in fellowship with himself.

The single aim of the blessing of Pentecost is to reveal Jesus as a Savior, so that He may exhibit His power to redeem souls here in the world. The Spirit did not simply come to occupy the place of Jesus, but came to unite the disciples with their Lord more closely, and deeply, and completely than when He was on earth. The power from on high did not come as a power which they were then to consider as their own: the power was inseparably bound up with the Lord Jesus and the Holy Spirit. Every operation of the power was a direct working of God in them. The fellowship which the disciples had with Jesus on earth, the following of Him, the reception of His teaching, the doing of His will, the participation in His suffering—all this was to still be their experience, only in greater measure.

It is the same with us. The Spirit in us will always glorify Jesus, will always make it manifest that He alone is to be Lord, that all which is glorious comes only from Him. Close communion with God in the inner chamber, faithfulness in searching His Word and seeking to know His will in the Scriptures, sacrifice of time and business and fellowship with others, to bring us into touch with the Savior—all this is indispensable for the keeping of the blessing. Jesus keeps us through our fellowship with Him, being occupied with himself. He that loves His fellowship above everything shall have the experience of His keeping.

Jesus maintains the blessing in the pathway of obedience.

When the Lord Jesus promised the Holy Spirit, He stated repeatedly that the blessing was for the obedient. "If ye love me, keep my commandments. And I will pray the Father, and he shall give you another Comforter" (John 14:15, 16, 21, 23). Peter speaks of "the Holy Ghost, whom God hath given to them that obey him" (Acts 5:32). Of our Lord himself we read that He "became obedient unto death . . . wherefore God also hath highly exalted him" (Phil. 2:8, 9). Obedience is what God cannot but demand. It is the only true relation and blessedness of the creature. It is obedience that attains what was lost by the Fall. It is the power of obedience that Jesus came to restore. It is His own life. Apart from obedience the blessing of Pentecost can neither come nor abide.

There are two kinds of obedience. There is one that is very defective, like that of the disciples previous to Pentecost. They desired from the heart to do what the Lord said, but they had not the power. Yet the Lord accounted their desire and purpose as obedience. On the other hand, there is a more abundant life, which comes with the fullness of the Spirit, where new power is given for full obedience. The characteristic of the full blessing of Pentecost, and the way to keep it, is a surrender to obedience in the minutest details. To listen to the voice of Jesus himself, to the voice of the Spirit, to the voice of conscience, this is the way in which Jesus leads us. The method of making the life of Pentecost within us sure and strong is to know Jesus and to love Him, and receive Him in that aspect which made Him well-pleasing to the Father—namely, as the Obedient One. The whole Jesus becomes the life of the soul.

It is the exercise of this obedience that gives to the soul a wonderful firmness and confidence and power to trust God and to expect all from Him. A strong will is necessary for a strong faith, and it is strengthened to trust God to the uttermost. This is the only way in which the Lord can lead us to ever richer blessing.

Jesus maintains the blessing in fellowship with His people.

The believer's initial seeking of the full blessing is usually for himself only. Even after he receives the blessing as a new experience, he is still rather disposed to maintaining it safely for himself. But the Spirit will quickly teach him that a member of the body cannot enjoy the flow of healthful life in a state of separation from others. He begins to understand that "there is one body and one Spirit." The unity of the body must be realized to enjoy the fullness of the Spirit.

This principle teaches some important lessons about the condition on which the blessing received can be maintained. All that you have belongs to others and must be employed for their service. All that they have belongs to you and is in turn indispensable for you. The Spirit of the body of the Lord can work effectively only when the members of it work in unison. You should confess to others what the Lord has done for you, ask their intercession, seek their fellowship, and help them with what the Lord has given you. You should consider the wretched condition of the Church in our days, yet not in the spirit of judgment or bitterness, but rather in the spirit of humility and prayer, of gentleness and willingness to serve. Jesus will teach you what is meant by the saying that "love is the greatest" (1 Cor. 13:13); and by the very intensity of your surrender to the welfare of His Church He will both keep and increase the blessing in you.

Jesus maintains the blessing in the service of His kingdom.

We have often stated that the Spirit came as the power for work. The very name of Jesus Christ involves entire consecration to God's work, utter devotion to the rescue of souls. It was for this cause that He lived: it is only for this that He lives in Heaven. How can anyone possibly dream of having the Spirit of Christ other than as the Spirit which aims at the work of God and the salvation of souls? It is an impossibility. It is vital, then, that we keep these two aspects of the Spirit's operation closely knit together. *What the Spirit works in us is for the sake of what He works by us.* Our seeking for the blessing will miscarry, our initial possession of the blessing will be lost, if we do not as the dominant feature of our life present ourselves to be used by the Spirit in the doing of His work.

The blessing of Pentecost does not always come with equal power and not always at once. God often gives preparatory experiences and awakenings that lead to the full blessing. Every attempt to keep such gracious gifts for ourselves will entail loss. He that does not follow his own inclinations, but presents himself to the Lord and waits upon Him with an undivided spirit, will experience that work of God which makes him effective and will be strengthened to maintaining the blessing.

One thought more. *It is as the indwelling Lord that Jesus maintains the blessing of Pentecost in us.*

Whenever mention is made of Jesus as our Keeper, it is often difficult to believe that we can really know ourselves to be always in His hands and under His power. How much clearer and more glorious does the truth become when the Spirit discovers to us that Christ is in us; and that indwelling is so united to us as to be compared to the soul in the body animating and moving every part of it. Yes: it is thus that Christ dwells in us, penetrating our whole nature with His nature. The Holy Spirit came for the purpose of making Him deeply present within us. As the sun is high above me, and yet by its heat penetrates my bones and marrow and quickens my whole life, so the Lord Jesus, who is exalted high in heaven, penetrates my whole nature by His Spirit in such a way that all my willing, and thinking, and feeling are animated by Him. We no longer think of an external person in heaven who is keeping us, but rather that our whole individual life is quickened and possessed by One who in a divine, all-penetrating manner occupies and fills the heart. Then we see how natural, how certain, how blessed it is that the indwelling Jesus keeps the blessing and always maintains the fullness of the Spirit.

Are you longing for this life in the fullness of blessing, and yet afraid to enter upon it because you do not know how to continue? Listen: Jesus will make this blessing continuous and sure. The blessing is this—that as Jesus Christ was daily with His disciples in bodily fashion, so He will by His Spirit every day and always be your life; yes, live His life in you. No one can fully understand how things look from the top of a mountain until he himself has been there. Although you do not understand everything, believe that the Lord Jesus has sent His Spirit to receive and keep you in His divine power. Trust Him for this. Let all burdens be laid aside, and receive from Him this full blessing of Pentecost as a fountain which He himself will cause to spring up in you unto everlasting life.

8

How It May Be Increased

"He that believeth on me shall never thirst" (John 6:35).
*"He that believeth on me . . . out of his belly shall flow
rivers of living water"* (John 7:38).

Can the full blessing of Pentecost be increased? Can
anything that is full become still fuller? Yes: undoubtedly.
It can become so full that it always overflows. This is especially the characteristic and law of the blessing of Pentecost.

The words of our blessed Lord Jesus point us to a double blessing. First, Jesus says that he who believes in Him
shall never thirst: he shall always have life in himself—
that is to say, the satisfaction of all his needs. Then He
speaks of something that is grander and more glorious: he
who believes in Him, out of his heart shall flow rivers of
living water to quench the thirst of others. It is the distinction between full and overflowing. A vessel may be

70

full and yet have nothing over for others. When it continues full, and yet has something over for others, there must be in it an over-brimming, ever-flowing supply. This is what our Lord promises to believers. At the outset, faith in Him gives them the blessing that they shall never thirst. But as they advance and become stronger in faith, it makes them a fountain of water out of which streams flow to others. The Spirit who at first only fills us will overflow out to souls around us.

The rivers of living water are similar to many fountains on earth. When we begin to open them, the stream is weak. The more the water is used, and the deeper the source is opened up, the stronger the water flows. I would like to explore this principle in the realm of the spiritual life and try to discover what is necessary that the fullness of the Spirit may flow more abundantly from us. There are several simple directions which may help us in reaching this knowledge.

Hold fast to what you have.

See to it that you do not misunderstand the blessing which God has given you. Be sure that you do not form any wrong conceptions of what the full blessing is. Do not imagine that the joy and power of Pentecost must be felt and seen immediately. No: the Church at present is in a dead-and-alive condition, and the restoration often comes slowly. At first, one receives the full blessing only as a seed: the full life is wrapped up in a little invisible capsule. The believer has longed for it; he has surrendered himself unreservedly for it; he has believed in silence that God has accepted his consecration and fulfilled His promise. In that faith he goes on his way, silent and happy, saying to himself: "The blessing of the fullness of the Spirit is for me." But the actual experiences of the blessing did not come as he had anticipated; or they did come, but lasted only for a short time. The result was that he began to fear that his surrender was not a reality; that he had been rejoicing in what was only a fleeting emotion; and that the real blessing was something greater and more powerful than he had yet received. The result is he moves further back rather than forward through discouragement on account of his disappointment.

The cause of this condition is simply lack of faith. We are bent on judging God and His work in us by sight and feeling. We forget that the whole process is the work of faith. Even in its highest revelations in Christians that have made the greatest progress, faith rests not on what is to be seen of the work of God or on the experiences of it, but on the work of God as spiritual, invisible, deeply hidden, and inconceivable. If you have gone into this time of discouragement and desire to return to the true life according to the promise, my counsel is to not be surprised if it comes to you slowly or if it appears to be involved in darkness. If you know that you have given yourself to God wholeheartedly, and if you know that God, really and with His whole heart, waits to fulfill His promise in you with divine power, then rest in silence before His face and hold fast your integrity. Although the cold of winter appears to bury everything in death, say with the prophet Habakkuk: "Although the fig-tree shall not blossom, neither shall fruit be in the vines . . . yet I will rejoice in the Lord, I will joy in the God of my salvation" (3:17, 18). Do this, and you will know God, and God will know you. If you have set yourself before God as an empty, separated, purified vessel, to become full of His Spirit, then continue to regard yourself so and keep silence before Him. If you have believed that God has received you to fill you as a purified vessel—purified through Jesus Christ and by your entire surrender to Him—then abide in this attitude day by day, and you may depend upon it that the blessing will grow and begin to flow. "He that believeth on him shall not be confounded" (Isa. 28:16; 1 Pet. 2:6).

Persevere in the entire denial of yourself and the sacrifice of everything.

If I wish to have a reservoir of water, the greater the excavation I make for it, the greater is the quantity of water I can collect, and the stronger is the stream that flows from it when the floodgates are opened. In your surrender for sanctification, or for the full blessing of the Spirit, you have said in truth and uprightness that you are prepared to sacrifice and forsake all in order to win this pearl of the kingdom of heaven; and this consecration was acceptable to God. But, perhaps you have not fully understood the words you have used. The Lord has still much to teach you concerning what the individual self is, how deeply it is rooted, how utterly corrupt as well as deeply hidden it is, as the secret source of many things you both say and do. Be willing to make room for the Spirit by a constant, daily, and entire denial of the self-life, and you may be sure that He will always be willing to come and fill the empty place. You have forsaken and sacrificed everything as far as you know; but keep your mind open to the Spirit, and He will lead you further on, and let you see that only when the entire sacrifice of everything after the example of Christ comes to be the rule in His Church shall the blessing again break forth like an overflowing stream.

It is surprising how sometimes a very little thing may hinder the continuing increase of the blessing. It may, for example, be a little variance between friends, in which they show that they are not willing to forgive according to the law of Christ. Or it may be some yielding to undue sensitiveness or to the ambition which is not prepared to take the servant role. Or it may be the possession or use of earthly property as if it were our own. Or it may be the enjoyment of eating and drinking without the self-denial which Christ expects at our hands every day. Or it may be in connection with things that are lawful and in themselves innocent, which however, do not reflect our profession of being led by the Spirit of God. Here, as our Lord did in His earthly ministry, we are bound to show that the heavenly portion we possess is itself sufficient to satisfy all our desires. Or it may be in connection with doubtful things, in which we give way too easily to the lust of the flesh.

Do you really desire to enjoy the full measure of the blessing of the Spirit? Then, before temptation comes, train yourself to understand the fundamental law of the imitation of Jesus and of full discipleship—*forsake all.* Allow yourself also to be strengthened and drawn into the observance of it by the sure promise of the "hundredfold in this life." A full blessing will be given you, a measure shaken together and running over.

Regard yourself as living only to make others happy.

God is love. His whole being is nothing but a surrender of himself in love to be the life of the creature, to make the creature participate in His holiness and blessedness. He blesses and serves all that lives. His glory as God is that He puts all that He has at the disposal of His creatures.

Jesus Christ is the Son of God's love, the Bearer, the Bringer, the Dispenser of the love. What God is as invisible in heaven, He was as visible on earth. He came, He lived, He suffered and died only to glorify the Father— that is, to let it be seen how glorious the Father in His love is, and to show that in the Godhead there is no other purpose than to bless men and make them happy; to make it manifest that the highest honor and blessedness of any being is to give and to sacrifice.

The Holy Spirit came as the Spirit of the Father and the Son to make us partakers of this divine nature, to shed abroad the love of God in our hearts, to secure the indwelling of the Son and His love in our hearts to such an extent that Christ may truly be formed within us, and that our whole "inner man" shall bear the impression of His character and His likeness.

When a believer seeks and receives the fullness of the Spirit, and desires to have it increased, is it not perfectly clear that he can enjoy this blessing only to the degree that he is prepared to give himself to the service of love? The Spirit comes to expel the life of self and self-seeking. The fullness of the Spirit presupposes a willingness to consecrate ourselves to the blessing of others and as the servants of all, and that in a constantly increasing and unreserved measure. The Spirit is the outflowing of the life of God. If we will but yield ourselves to Him, He will become rivers of living water, flowing from the depths of our heart.

The secret to having the blessing increased is to begin to live as a man who is left here on earth only in order that the love of God may work through you. Love all around you with the love of God which is in you through the Spirit. Love the children of God cordially, even the weakest and most despised. Exercise and exhibit your love in every possible way. Love the unsaved. Present yourself to the Spirit to love Him. Then will love constrain you to speak, to work, to give, and to pray. If there is no open door for working, or if you have not the strength for it, the door of prayer is always open, and power can be obtained at the mercy seat. Embrace the whole world in your love; for Christ, who is in your heart, belongs also to the heathen. The Spirit is the power of Christ for redeeming them. Like God and Jesus and the Spirit, live wholly to bless others. Then the blessing shall stream forth and become overflowing.

Let Jesus Christ be everything for your faith.
You know what the Scripture says: "It pleased the Father that in him should all fulness dwell" (Col. 1:20); and

again: "All the promises of God in him are yea, and in him Amen, unto the glory of God by us" (2 Cor. 1:20). When the Lord spoke of "rivers of living water," He connected the promise with faith in himself: "He that believeth in me, out of his heart shall flow rivers." If we understand that word "believeth," we would require no other answer than this to the question as to how the blessing may be increased.

Faith is primarily a seeing by the Spirit that Jesus is a flowing fountain of the divine love, and that the Spirit himself always flows from Him as the Bearer of the life that this love brings and that always streams forth in love. Then it is an embracing of the promise, an appropriation of the blessing as it is provided in Christ, a resting in the certainty of it, and a thanking of God for what He is yet to do. Faith is a keeping open of the soul, so that Christ can come in with the blessing and take possession and fill all. Faith becomes the most fervent and unbroken communion between the soul in which Christ obtains His place and Christ himself, who by the silent, effectual blessing of the Spirit is enthroned in the heart.

Believers must learn the lesson that, if you believe, you shall see the glory of God. Let every doubt, every weakness, every temptation find you trusting, rejoicing in Jesus, and depending upon His always working in you. You know that there are two ways to encounter and strive against sin. One is to endeavor to ward it off with all your might, seeking strength in the Word and in prayer. In this form of the conflict we use the power of the will. The other is to turn at the very moment of the temptation to the Lord Jesus in the silent exercise of faith and say to Him: "Lord, I have no strength. You are my Keeper" (Ps. 121:5). This is the method of faith. "This is the victory that overcometh the world, even our faith" (1 John 5:4). Yes: this is indeed "the one thing needful," because it is the only way in which Jesus, who is in himself "The One Thing

Needful," can maintain the work of His Spirit in us. It is by the exercise of faith without ceasing that the blessing will flow without ceasing.

Christ must be all to us every moment. It is of no avail to me that I have life on earth unless that life is renewed every moment by my inbreathing of fresh air. Even so must God actually renew, and uphold, and strengthen the divine life in me every moment. He does this for me in my union with Christ. Christ is the fullness of God, the life of God, the love of God prepared for us and communicating itself to us. The Spirit is the fullness of Christ, the life of Christ, the self-communicating love of Christ, surrounding us as the air surrounds the body.

Oh, let us believe that we are in Christ, who surrounds us in His heavenly power, longing to make the rivers of His Spirit flow forth by us! Let us endeavor to obtain a heart filled with the joyful assurance that the Almighty Lord will fulfill His word with power, and that our only choice is to see Him, to rejoice in Him, and sacrifice all for Him. Then shall His word become true: "He that believeth in me, out of his heart shall flow rivers of living water." Amen.

9

How It Comes to Its Full Manifestation

"I bow my knees unto the Father"—

1. *"That he would grant you . . . to be strengthened with might by his Spirit in the inner man;*

2. *That Christ may dwell in your hearts by faith;*

3. *That ye, being rooted and grounded in love, may be able to comprehend . . . the love of Christ which passeth knowledge;*

4. *That ye might be filled with all the fulness of God"* (Eph. 3:14–19).

We have remarked often that every blessing which God gives is like a seed with the power of an indissoluble life hidden in it. Let no one therefore imagine that to be filled with the Spirit is a condition of perfectness which leaves nothing more to be desired. This is not true in any sense. It was after the Lord Jesus was filled with the Spirit that

78

He had to be still further perfected by temptations and the learning of obedience. When the disciples were filled with the Spirit on the day of Pentecost, this equipment with power from on high was given to them that they might carry out the victory over sin in their own lives and all around them. The Spirit is the Spirit of truth, and He must guide us into it. It will only be by slow degrees that He will lead us into the eternal purpose of God, into the knowledge of Christ, into true holiness, into full fellowship with God. The fullness of the Spirit is simply the full preparation for living and working as a child of God.

From this point of view we see at a glance how indispensable it is for every believer to aim at obtaining this blessing. Then we begin to realize that this is the very blessing that we should encourage the weak and timid to accept. We also understand why it is that Paul offers this prayer in behalf of all believers without distinction. He did not regard it as a spiritual distinction or special luxury which was intended only for those who were prominent or favored among believers. No: it was for all without distinction, for all who at their conversion had by faith received the Holy Spirit, that he prayed. And his request was that by the special, powerful, and ever-deepening work of the Spirit, God would bring them to their true destiny—to be filled unto all the fullness of God. This prayer of Paul is everywhere regarded as one of the most glorious representations that the Word of God gives of what the Christian life should be. Let us then endeavor to learn what the full revelation and manifestation of this blessing of the Spirit may become.

That the Father would grant you to be strengthened with power through the Spirit.

That these Christians had received the Spirit when they believed in Christ is clear from a previous statement (Eph. 1:14). But he sees that they do not yet know or have all that the Spirit can do for them, and that there is a danger that, by their ignorance, they may make no further progress. Therefore he bows his knees and prays without ceasing that the Father would strengthen them with power by His Spirit in the inner man. This powerful strengthening with the Spirit is equivalent to being filled with the Spirit, is indeed this same blessing under another aspect. It is the indispensable condition of a healthful, growing, and fruitful life.

Paul prays that the Father would grant this. He asks for a new, definite operation of God. He entreats that God would do this *according to the riches of His glory*. It is surely not a small thing, anything very common, that he desires. He desires that God remember and bring into play all the riches of His grace and, in a fashion consistent with the divine glory of His power, do a heavenly wonder and, as the living God, strengthen these believers with might by His Spirit in the inner man.

Believer, learn that your daily life depends on God's will, on God's grace, on God's omnipotence. Yes: every moment God must work in your inner life and strengthen you by His Spirit, otherwise you cannot live as He would have you live. Just as no creature in the natural world can exist for a moment if God does not work in it to sustain its life, so the gift of the Holy Spirit is the pledge that God himself is to work everything in us from moment to moment. Learn to know your entire, your blessed dependence on God, and the claim which you have on your Heavenly Father to begin in you a life in the mighty strengthening of the Spirit and to maintain it without the interruption of a single moment.

Paul tells these believers what he prays for in their behalf in order that they may know what they have need of and ask it for themselves. Have you also learned to ask for yourself? Expect everything from God alone. Bow your knees, and ask and expect from the Father that He would manifest to you—yes, in you—the riches of His glory. Ask and expect that He will strengthen you with might by His Spirit, that Spirit who in fact is already in you. Let this become the one desire, the strong confidence of your soul: "God will fill me with the Spirit: God will strengthen me through the Spirit with His Almighty energy." Let your whole life be permeated daily by this prayer and this expectation.

That Christ may dwell in your hearts by faith.

This is the glorious fruit of the divine strengthening with power in the inner man by the Spirit. The great work of the Father in eternity is to bring forth the Son.

In Him alone is the good pleasure of God realized. The Father can have no fellowship with the creature except through the Son. He can have no joy in it except as He beholds His Son in it. Therefore it is His great work in redemption to reveal His Son in us, and so to obtain a dwelling place for Him in us, that *our life be a visible expression of the life of Jesus.*

That is His goal in strengthening us with power by the Spirit in the inner man. It is that Christ may dwell in our hearts by faith.

This indwelling of Christ is not like that of a man who lives in a house, but is nevertheless in no sense identified with it. No: His indwelling is a possession of our hearts that is truly divine, quickening and penetrating our inmost being with His life. The Father strengthens us inwardly with might by His Spirit, so that the Spirit animates our will and brings it, like the will of Jesus, into entire agreement with His own. The result is that our heart then, like the heart of Jesus, bows before Him in humility and surrender; our life seeks only His honor; and our whole soul thrills with desire and love for Jesus. This inward renewal makes the heart a proper dwelling place of the Lord. By the Spirit He is revealed within us and we come to know that He is actually in us as our life, in a deep, divine unity, One with us.

Believer, God longs to see Jesus in you. He is prepared to work mightily in you that Christ may dwell in you. The Spirit has come, and the Father is willing to work mightily by Him, that the living presence of His Son may always abide in you. Jesus loves you so dearly and longs so intensely for you that He cannot rest until He makes His abode in your heart. This is the supreme blessing that the fullness of the Spirit brings you.

That Christ may dwell in your heart by faith. It is by faith that you receive and know the indwelling of the Spirit and the operation of the Father through Him. By faith, which discerns things invisible as clearly as the sun, you receive and know the living Jesus in your heart. As constantly as He was with His disciples on earth—yes, more constantly than with them, because more inwardly and more really—He will be in you and will grant you to enjoy His presence and His love. Pray that the Father would strengthen you with might by the Spirit, would open your heart for the fullness of the Spirit, and enable you trustfully to appropriate it. Then at last you will know what it means to have Christ dwelling in your heart by faith.

That you, being rooted and grounded in love, may be strong to know the love of Christ which passeth knowledge.

Here is the glorious fruit of the indwelling of Christ in the heart. By the Spirit the love of God is shed abroad in the heart. By Christ who dwells in the heart the love whereby God loved Him comes into us; and we learn that just as the life between the Father, Son, and Spirit is only infinite love, so the life of Christ in us is nothing but love. Thus we become rooted and grounded in love. We are implanted in the soil of love; we strike our roots into heavenly love; we have our being in it and draw our strength from it. Love is the supreme element in our spiritual life.

The Spirit in us and the Son in us bring us nothing but the love of God. Love is the first and the chief among the streams of living water that are to flow from us.

We come to discover the truth that love is the fulfilling of the law; that love does no evil to one's neighbor (Rom. 13:10); that love seeks not its own (1 Cor. 13:5); that love lays down its life for the brethren (1 John 3:16). Our heart becomes ever larger and larger; our friends and our enemies, the children of God and the children of the world, those that are worthy to be loved and those that are hateful, the world as a whole and every individual creature in particular—are all embraced in the love of God. We find, then, our happiness lies in the sacrifice of our own honor, our own advantage and comfort, in favor of others. Love takes no account of sacrifice: it is its blessedness to love: it cannot do otherwise; actual loving is its nature and its life. We are enabled to love because the Father with His Spirit works mightily within us; because the Son, "who loved me and gave himself for me," dwells in us, and He, who is crucified Love, has filled the heart completely with himself. We are rooted in love, and in accordance with the nature of the root in God is the fruit from God—love.

That you may be strong to know the love which passes knowledge: that is, to know love not with the knowledge of the understanding and its thoughts alone, but in the conscious blessedness of a heart in which Jesus dwells; to know love as something that cannot be known or conceived by the heart of itself; to be strong to know it fully, so far as this is possible before God, in order that He may fill you, an earthen vessel, with His own love to overflowing.

Listen to the word: "God is love"; and He has provided everything to the end that you may know love fully. It is for this object that the Spirit is in you, and that the Father will work mightily in you: it is with this aim that Christ desires to have your whole heart. Oh, let us begin to pray, as never before, that the Father would strengthen us with power by the Spirit; that the Father would grant us to be filled with the Spirit; that we may be strong to know the love of Christ.

That you may be filled unto all the fullness of God.
What an expression! what an impenetrable mystery! what a divine blessedness! *Filled* unto all the fullness of God: this is the experience to which the fullness of the Spirit is intended to bring us, and will bring us.

Filled unto all the *fullness* of God: who shall ever unfold the meaning of this expression to us? Shall we ever comprehend what it signifies? God has made provision for our enlightenment. In Christ Jesus we see a man full of God, a man who was perfected by suffering and obedience, filled unto all the fullness of God; yes, a man who in the solitariness and poverty of an ordinary human life, with all its needs and infirmities, has nevertheless allowed us to see on earth the life enjoyed by the inhabitants of heaven, as they are there filled unto all the fullness of God. The will and the honor, the love and the service of God were always visible in Him. God was all to Him.

When God called the world into existence, it was in order that it might reveal Him. In it His wisdom and power and goodness were to dwell and be visibly manifested. We say continually that God can be seen everywhere in nature. The Seraphim sing: the whole earth is full of His glory. When God created man after His image, it was in order that He himself might be seen in man, that man should simply serve as a reflection of His likeness. The image of a man never serves any other purpose than to represent the man. As the image of God man was destined to simply receive the glory of God in his own life, to bear it and make it visible. God was to be all to him, to be all in him: he was to be full of God.

By sin this divine purpose has been frustrated. Instead

of being full of God, man became full of himself and the world; and to such an extent has sin blinded us that it appears an impossibility ever to become full of God again. Alas! even many believers see nothing desirable in this fullness. Yet it is to this blessing that Jesus came to redeem and bring us; and this is the end for which God is prepared to work mightily within us by His Spirit. This is no less the result for which the Son of God desires to dwell in our heart, and which He will bring to accomplishment: it is that we may be filled unto the fullness of God.

Yes, this is the highest aim of the Pentecostal blessing. To attain this, we can count upon the Spirit's ministry. He will open the way for us and guide us in it. He will work in us the deep humility of Jesus, who always said: "I can of mine own self do *nothing*"; "I came . . . *not* to do mine own will"; I have *not* spoken of myself" (John 5:30; 6:38; 12:49; 14:10). Amid this self-emptying and sense of dependence, He will work in us the assurance and the experience that for the soul which is nothing, God is surely ALL. By our faith He will reveal to us Jesus, who was full of God, as our life. He will cause us to be rooted in the love in which God gives all, and we shall take God as all. Thus it will be with us as with Jesus: man nothing, and God's honor, God's will, God's love, God's power—everything. Yes, the issue will be that we shall be "filled unto all the fullness of God."

Believer, I beg of you by the love of God not to say that this is too high an experience for you, or that it is not for you. No, it is in truth the will of God concerning you: the will both of His commandment and of His promise. He will fulfill His promise. He himself will work it out. Today, then, in humility and faith take this word, "FILLED UNTO ALL THE FULLNESS OF GOD," as the purpose and the watchword of your life, and see what it will do for you. It will become a powerful lever to raise you out of the self-seeking which is quite content with only being prepared for blessing. It will urge you to enter into and become firmly rooted in the love of God which gives everything to you, and thereby in the love which gives everything back to Him. It will convince you that nothing less than Christ himself dwelling in your heart can keep such a love abiding in you, or actually make the fullness of God a reality within you. It will train you to fix your only hope on the mighty operation of God himself by the Spirit. It will also move you to go down upon your knees and summon to your aid the wealth of God's glory that it may itself prepare you for this great wonder. This it will continue to do until your heart is enabled to utter the response: "Yes: FILLED UNTO ALL THE FULLNESS OF GOD is what my God has prepared for me."

With this glorious prospect before us, let us join with the apostle in the doxology: "Unto him that is able to do exceeding abundantly above all that we ask or think, according to the power that worketh in us, unto him be glory . . . throughout all ages" (Eph. 3:20, 21). Let us desire nothing less than these riches of the glory of God. Today, if we have never done it before, make a beginning and appropriate to yourself the full blessing of the Spirit as the power which is sure to lead us to be "filled unto all the fullness of God."

When God said to Abraham, "I am God Almighty," He invited him to trust His omnipotence to fulfill His promise. When Jesus went down into the grave and its impotence, it was in the faith that God's omnipotence could lift Him to the throne of His glory. It is that same omnipotence that waits to work out God's purpose in them that believe in Him to do so. Let our hearts say, "Unto him *THAT IS ABLE* to do exceeding abundantly above all that we ask or think . . . unto him be glory." Amen.

10

How Fully It Is Assured to Us by God

"If ye then, being evil, know how to give good gifts unto your children, how much more shall your heavenly Father give the Holy Spirit to them that ask him?" (Luke 11:13).

When Jairus came to Jesus to entreat His help for his dying daughter and then learned that she had already died, Jesus said: "Fear not: believe only" (Luke 8:50). Face-to-face with a sorrow in which he was utterly helpless, the Lord called upon Jairus to put his trust in himself. There was but one thing that could help him: "only believe." Countless times this word has been the strength of God's children, where humanly speaking all hope was lost and success appeared to be impossible. We who are desiring to know the full Pentecostal blessing have need of this same word. The inconceivable preciousness of the blessing and of the divine element in it indeed proves that only the wonder-working power of God can make this exceeding grace a reality within us. Let us also be silent before God; here we shall hear the voice of Jesus saying to us: "Fear not: believe only": God will do it for you.

This divine assurance was clearly stated by Jesus' word that much more readily than an earthly father will give his children bread will God give the Holy Spirit to them that ask Him. We regard it as child abuse on the part of a father if he does not feed his children; how much more, then, shall not God give the promised fullness of the Spirit to those that ask Him. In the midst of all the aspects of our spiritual life, the fundamental element must be the firm confidence that the Father will give His child His full heritage. God is spirit. He desires in His eternal love to obtain full possession of us; but He can accomplish this only by giving us His Spirit. As surely as He is God will He fill you with His Holy Spirit. Without that faith you will never succeed in receiving this blessing. That faith will give you the victory over every difficulty. Therefore, "fear not: only believe." Hear the voice of Jesus: "Said I not unto thee that if thou believest thou shalt see the glory of God?"

Let us listen to these three great lessons.

1. *Although you cannot comprehend or explain everything by the mere power of your understanding, still: "only believe."*

There are many preliminary questions which immediately arise in connection with this subject, and our temptation is to attempt to understand everything about it before we expect the blessing. Two of these questions I will mention now.

The first is: does this blessing come from *within* or from *above*? Some believers immediately say that it must come from *within*. The Holy Spirit descended upon the earth on the day of Pentecost and was given to the Christian community. At the moment of conversion He comes into our heart. We have therefore no longer to pray that He may be given to us: we must simply recognize and use what we already have. We should not seek to have more of the Spirit: we have Him in the fullness of the gift as it is. It is rather the Holy Spirit who must have more of us. As we yield ourselves entirely to Him He will entirely fill us. It is from *within* that the blessing must come: the fountain of living water is already there; the fountain has only to be open and every obstruction cleared and the water shall stream forth. It must spring from *within*.

On the other hand, other believers say, "No, it must come from *above*. *When, on the day of Pentecost, the Father bestowed the Spirit, He did not give Him away beyond His own control. The fullness of the Spirit still remains in God. God bestows nothing apart from himself, to work without or independently of His will. He himself works only through the Spirit and every new and greater manifestation of the Spirit's power comes directly from above.* Years after the day of Pentecost the Spirit came down again from heaven at Samaria and Caesarea. In His fullness He is in heaven still; and it is from God in heaven that the fullness of the Spirit is to be sought.

Dear believer, please do not waste your time deciding which of these is the right one. God blesses men in both camps. When the flood came all the fountains of the abyss were broken up and the gates of heaven were opened. It came simultaneously from beneath and from above. God is prepared to bless men in both camps. He desires to teach us to know and honor the Spirit who is already within us. He also desires to bring us to wait upon himself in a spirit of utter dependence, and to beseech Him that He as our Father would give us our daily bread, the new, the fuller influx of His Spirit. Do not allow yourself to be held back by this question. *God understands your petition.* He knows what you desire. Believe that God is prepared to fill you with His Spirit; let that faith look up to Him with unceasing prayer and confidence. He will give the blessing.

The other question is: Does this blessing come gradually or at once? Will it be a silent, unobserved increase of the grace of the Spirit or a momentary, explosive outpouring of His power? Here again, we find that God has already sent this blessing in both modes, and will continue to do so. What must take place at once is this: there must be a definite decision to unreservedly surrender your life to the control of the Spirit, and a conviction of faith that God has accepted this. In the majority of cases this is done at once. It must finally come to this, perhaps after a long period of seeking and praying, that the soul shall present itself to God for this blessing in one definite, irrevocable act, and believes that the offering is then sanctified and accepted upon the altar. Then, whether the experience of the blessing comes at once and with power, or comes quietly and gradually, the soul must maintain its act of self-dedication and simply look to God to do His own work.

Thus in dealing with all such questions the chief concern is this: *"only believe" and rest in the faithfulness of God.* Hold fast this one principle: God has promised that He will fill us with His Spirit. It is His work to make His promise an accomplished fact. Thank God for the promise even as you would thank Him for the fulfillment of it. In the promise God has already pledged himself to you. Rejoice in Him and in His faithfulness. Refuse to play reasoning games about it. Set your heart on what God will do, on himself from whom the blessing must come. The result will be certain and glorious.

2. *Although you receive but little help from others, or even encounter opposition, still: "only believe."*
One of the saddest tokens of the unspiritual condition of the Church is that so many are content with things just as they are, and have no desire to know more of the reality

of the Spirit's power. They point to the present purity of
doctrine, to the prevailing earnestness of preaching, to the
generous gifts made to the Church, to the interest manifested in the cause of education and of missions, and they
say that we ought rather to give God thanks for the good
we see around us. Such people would condemn the lan-
guage of Laodicea, and would refuse to say that they were
rich and increased in goods and had need of nothing (Rev.
3:17), and yet there are traces of this spirit in what they
say. They do not consider the injunction to be "filled with
the Spirit." They have forgotten the command to prophesy
to the Spirit and say: "Come from the four winds, O breath,
and breathe upon the slain, that they may live" (Ezek.
37:9). When you speak of these things, you will receive
little encouragement from them. They do not understand
what you mean. They believe in the Holy Spirit, but they
do not see that the fullness of the Spirit is the one thing
needful for the Church.

Others will agree with you when you speak of this need,
and yet will really give you even less encouragement. They
have often both thought and prayed over the matter, but
have made no real progress. They look to the Church of
earlier times and say that it was never much different
than it is now. What you say of the impotence of the Church
in its relations to the world is true; your representation
of the promise of God is glorious; all that you expect from
the mighty working of the Spirit is the highest degree
desirable; but—it is not to be obtained. These people be-
long to the generation of the ten spies who were sent to
spy out Canaan: the land is glorious, but the enemy in
possession is too strong; we are too weak to overcome them.
Lack of consecration and of willingness to surrender
everything for this blessing is the root of the unbelief, and
has made them incapable of exercising the courage of
Caleb: "Let us go up at once, and possess it; for we are
well able to overcome it" (Num. 13:20).

If you desire to be filled with the Spirit, do not allow yourself to be held back by such reasonings. "Only believe" and strengthen yourself in the omnipotence of God. Do not say: is God able? Say rather: *God is able*. The God who *was able* to raise Christ from the dead is still mighty in the midst of His people, and *is able* to reveal His divine life with power in your heart. Hear His voice saying to you as to Abraham: "I am the God Almighty: walk before me, and be thou perfect" (Gen. 17:1). Set your heart without distraction on what God has said that He will do, and then on the omnipotence which is prepared to bring the promise to accomplishment. Pray that the Father would grant you to be strengthened with might by His Spirit. Adore Him who is able to do for us exceeding abundantly above all that we ask or think, and give Him the glory. Let faith in the omnipotence of God fill your soul and you will be full of the assurance that, however difficult, however improbable, however impossible it may seem, God can fill us with His Spirit. "Only believe."

3. *Although everything in you appears entirely unfit for this blessing and unworthy of it, still: "only believe."*

When one prays for this blessing of being filled with the Spirit, the thought comes as to what one's life as a Christian has already been. The believer thinks of all the workings of divine grace in his heart, and of the incessant strivings of the Spirit. He thinks of all his efforts and prayers, of his past attempts at entire surrender and the appropriation of faith. He looks at what he is at the moment, upon his unfaithfulness and sin and helplessness, and he loses heart. So little progress has been made. The past testifies only of failure and unfaithfulness. Why think that the future will be any better? If all his praying and believing of earlier days have been of so little avail, why should he hope that everything is to be transformed at once? He sets up an image of the life of a man full of the

Holy Spirit, and alongside it he sets his own life as he knows it, and it becomes impossible for him to imagine that he shall ever be able to live as a man full of the Spirit. For such a task he is completely unable and feels no courage to make the attempt.

Believer, when such thoughts as these throng in upon you, there is but one counsel to follow, and that is: "only believe." Cast yourself into the arms of your Father who gives His children the Holy Spirit much more readily than an earthly father gives bread. *Only believe, and count upon the love of God.* All your self-dedication and surrender, all your faith and integrity is not a work by which you have to move God or make Him willing to bless you. Far from it. It is God that desires to bless you, and that will himself work everything in you. *God loves you as a father* and sees that, to be able to live in perfect health and happiness as His child, you need but one thing—to be full of His Spirit. Jesus has by His blood opened the way to the full enjoyment of this love. You must learn to enter into this love, to abide in this love, and by faith to acknowledge that it shines upon you and surrounds you, even as the light of the sun illumines and animates your body. Begin to trust this love. I do not say in its willingness: no—in its unspeakable longing to fill you entirely with itself. It is your Father whose love waits to make you full of His Spirit. He himself will do it for you.

And what does He desire from you? Simply this, that you yield yourself to Him in utter unworthiness, nothingness, and impotence, to let Him do this work in you. He is prepared to take charge of all the preparatory work. You may be sure that He will help you by His Spirit. He will strengthen you with might in the inner man, silently and hiddenly, yet nonetheless surely, to abandon everything that has to be given up and to receive this treasure. He will help you in the faith of appropriation to rest in His word and to wait for Him; and He will hold himself responsible for all the future. He will make provision that you shall be able to walk in the fullness of this blessing.

Perhaps you have already formed a very high idea of what a man must be that is filled with the Spirit and see no chance of your being able to measure up to it. Or maybe you have not been able to form any idea of it whatever, and are on that account afraid to strive for a life which is so unknown to you. Abandon all such thoughts. The Spirit alone, when He is once in you, will himself teach you what that life is, for He will work it in you. God will take upon himself the responsibility of making you full of the Spirit, not as a treasure which *you* must carry and keep, but as a power which is to carry and keep you. Therefore, "only believe": count upon the love of your Father.

In His promise of the blessing and the power of the Spirit the Lord Jesus always pointed to God the Father. He called it "the promise of the Father" (Luke 24:49). He directed us to the faithfulness of God: "He is faithful that promised" (Heb. 10:23). He directed us to the power of God: the Spirit was, as power from on high, to come from God himself (Acts 1:8). He directed us to the love of God: it is as a Father that God is to give this gift to His children. Let every thought of this blessing, and every desire for it only lead us to God. Here is something that He must do, that He must give, that He, He alone, must work. Let us in silent adoration set our heart upon God: He will do something for us. Let us joyfully trust in Him: He is able to do above all praying and thinking. His love will, oh so willingly, bestow upon us a full blessing. Therefore, "only believe": God will make me full of the Spirit. And say humbly: "Behold the handmaid of the Lord; be it unto me according to thy word" (Luke 1:38). "Faithful is he that calleth you, who also will do it."

11

How It Is Found by All

"Then will I sprinkle clean water upon you, and ye shall be clean: from all your filthiness, and from all your idols, will I cleanse you. And I will put my Spirit within you, and cause you to walk in my statutes, and ye shall keep my judgments, and do them" (Ezek. 36:25, 27).

The full Pentecostal blessing is for all the children of God. *As many* as are led by the Spirit of God, they are the children of God (Rom. 8:14). God does not give a half portion to any of His children. To every one He says: "Son, thou art ever with me, and all that I have is thine" (Luke 15:31). Christ is not divided; he that receives Him receives Him in all His fullness. Every believer is destined by God, and is actually called, to be filled with the Spirit.

In the preceding chapters I have had in special view those who are to some extent acquainted with these things, and have been already in search of the fullness of the

Spirit. But it is quite conceivable that some who read this book may have heard very little of the full Pentecostal blessing, and yet in their hearts the desire has risen to obtain a share in it. There is, however, so much that they have not as yet understood that they desire the simplest possible instructions—where they are to begin, and what they have to do—in order to succeed in their desire. They are prepared to acknowledge that their life is under the dominion of sin, and that it seems that they would have to strive long and earnestly to become full of the Spirit. I would like to inspire them with fresh courage and direct them to the God who has said: "I the Lord will hasten it in his time" (Isa. 60:22). I would like to give simple instructions from God's Word as to what the disposition and the attitude must be in which they can receive this blessing.

1. *There must be a new discovery and confession and casting away of sin.*

In the message of Ezekiel, God first promised: "I will cleanse you," and then: "I will put my Spirit within you." A vessel into which anything precious is to be poured must always first be cleansed. So, if the Lord is to give you a new and full blessing, a new cleansing must also take place. In your conversion, it is true, there was a confession and putting away of sin. Yet, the soul was still half enveloped in darkness: it thought more of its heinous sins and the punishment to come. Inward sin was hardly thought of. After conversion, effort was made to overcome sin, but to no avail. It did not know in what holiness the Lord desires His people to live; it did not know how pure and holy the Lord would have it be and would make it be.

This new cleansing must come through new confession and discovery of sin. The old leaven cannot be purged away unless it is first searched for and found. Do not assume that you already know sufficiently well that sin is in your life. Sit down in silent meditation with the express purpose of God exposing what your life really is like. How much pride, self-seeking, worldliness, self-will, and impurity is in it? Can such a heart receive the fullness of the Spirit? It is impossible. Consider your home life with wife and children, parents and friends—does temper, anxiety, bitterness, idle or harsh or unkind words testify how little you have been cleansed? Consider your life in the Church— is your religion merely intellectual, or formal, or people-pleasing, without the real humiliation of spirit, that real desire for the living God, that real love for Jesus, that real subjection to the Word, which constitute worship in spirit and in truth? Consider your general way of life—do the people among whom you work testify that they have observed, by your honorable spirit and disinterestedness and freedom from worldly-mindedness, that you are one who has been cleansed from sin by God? Contemplate all this in the light of what God expects from you and has offered to work in you, and take your place as a one who must be cleansed before God can bestow the full blessing.

This discovery must be followed by the actual putting away of what is impure. You must come with these sins, and especially with those that are most strictly your own besetting sins, and acknowledge them before God in confession, and there and then make renunciation of them. You must be brought to the conviction that your life is a guilty and shameful life. You are not at liberty to excuse it because you are so weak, or that the majority of believers live no higher life. You must resolve that your life is to undergo a complete transformation. The sins that still cleave to you are to be cast off and done away with.

Perhaps you say that you find yourself unable to cast them off. I say that you are quite able to do this; and in this way. You can give these sins up to God. If there is something in my house that I wish to have taken away and I myself am unable to carry it, I call for men who will do it for me and I give it over into their hands, saying: "Look here: take that away," and they do it. So I am able to say that I have put this thing out of my house. In like manner you can give up to God those sins of yours, against which you feel yourself utterly impotent. You can give them up to Him to be dealt with as He desires and He will fulfill His promise: "I will cleanse you from all your filthiness." There is nothing so needful as that there should be a very definite understanding between you and the Lord, that you on your part really confess your sin and give it up, and that you wait on Him until He assures that He has taken it, or rather has taken your heart and life, into His own hands to give you a complete victory.

2. *In this way you come to a new discovery, and reception, and experience of what Christ is and is prepared to do for you.*

If the knowledge of sin at conversion is superficial, so also is the faith in Jesus. Our faith, our reception of Jesus never goes further or deeper than our insight into sin. If since your conversion you have learned to know the inner power of sin, you are now prepared to receive from God a discovery of the inward invincible power of the Lord Jesus in your heart, such as you have never dreamed possible. If you truly desire a complete deliverance from sin, so as to be able to live in obedience to God, God will reveal the Lord Jesus to you as a complete Savior. He will make you know that, although the flesh and its desires always remains in you, the Lord Jesus will so dwell in your heart that the power of the flesh shall be kept in subjection by Him in order that you may no longer do the will of the flesh. Through Jesus Christ, God will so cleanse you from all unrighteousness, that day by day you may walk before God with a pure heart. What you really need is the discovery that He is prepared to work this change in you, and that you may receive it by faith, here and now.

Yes: this is what Jesus Christ desires to work in you by the Holy Spirit. He came to put away sin; not the guilt and punishment of it only, but sin itself. He has not only mastered the power and dominion of the law and its curse over you, but has also completely broken and taken away the power and dominion of sin. He has completely rescued you as a newborn soul from beneath the power of sin; and He lives in His heavenly authority and all-pervading presence in order to work out this deliverance in you. In this power He will live in you and himself carry out His work in you. As the indwelling Christ, He is bent on maintaining and manifesting His redemption in you. The sins which you have confessed, the pride and the lovelessness, the worldly-mindedness and vanity and all uncleanness, He will by His power take out of your heart; so that, although the flesh may tempt you, the choice and the joy of your heart abide in Him and in His obedience to God's will. Yes: you may indeed become "more than conqueror" through Him that loved you (Rom. 8:37). As the indwelling Christ, He will overcome sin in you.

What then is required on our side? Only this, that when you see that Jesus will carry out this work, you then open the door before Him and receive Him into the heart as Lord and King. Yes: that can be done at once. A house that has remained closely shut for twenty years can be penetrated by the light in a moment if the doors and windows are thrown open. In like manner, a heart that has remained enveloped in darknes and impotence for twenty years, because it did not know that Jesus was willing to take the victory over sin into His own hands, can have its whole experience changed in a moment. When it acknowledges its sinful condition and yields itself to God, and believes that the Son of God is prepared to assume the responsibility of the inner life and its purification from sin; when it ventures to trust the Lord that He will do this work at that very moment; then it may firmly believe that it is done, and that Jesus takes all that is in me into His own hands.

This is an act of faith that must be held to in faith. When doors and windows are thrown open, and the light streaming in drives out the darkness, we discover at once how much dust and impurity there is in the house. But the light shines that we may see how to take it away. When we receive Christ into the heart everything is not yet perfected: light and gladness are not seen and experienced at once; but by faith the soul knows that He who is faithful will keep His word and will surely do His work. The faith that has up to this moment only sought and wrestled, now rests in the Lord and His Word. *It knows that what was begun by faith must be carried forward only by faith.* It says: "I abide in Jesus; I know that He abides in me and that He will manifest himself to me." As Jesus cleansed the lepers with a word, and it was only when they were on their way to the priest that they found out they were clean, so He cleanses us by His Word. He that firmly holds that fact in faith will see the proofs of it.

3. *The soul is then prepared to receive the full blessing of the Spirit.*

The Lord first gave the promise, *I will cleanse you;* and then the second promise, *I will put my Spirit within you.* The Holy Spirit cannot fill the heart and continue to dwell in it unless a special and complete cleansing first takes place within it. The Spirit and sin are engaged in a mortal combat. The reason that the Spirit is restrained in the Church is sin, which is all too little known or dreaded or cast out. Men do not believe in the power of Christ to cleanse; and therefore He cannot do His work of baptizing with the Spirit. It is from Christ that the Spirit comes, and to Christ the Spirit returns again. It is the heart that gives Christ liberty to exercise dominion in it that shall inherit the full blessing. Therefore, if you have understood the lesson of this chapter, and have done what has been suggested to you; if you have believed in Jesus as the Lord that cleanses you and dwells in you to keep you clean, be assured that God will certainly fulfill His word: "I will cleanse you *and put my Spirit within you.*" Cleave to Jesus, who cleanses you: let Him be all within you; God will see to it that you are filled with the Spirit.

Only keep in view these two truths.

First, that the gift and the fullness of the Spirit do not always come, as on the day of Pentecost, with external observation. God is often a God that hides himself. Do not be surprised, therefore, if your heart does not at once feel as you should like it to feel immediately after your act of surrender or appropriation. Rest assured that if you fully trust Christ to do everything for you, He there and then begins to do it in secret by His Spirit. Count upon it that if you present yourself to God as a pure vessel, cleansed by Christ, to be filled with the Spirit, God will take you at your word and say unto you: "Receive ye the Holy Ghost" (John 20:22). At that moment bow down before Him, more and more silently, more and more deeply, in holy adoration and expectation, in the blessed assurance that the unseen God has now begun to carry on His work more mightily in you, and that He will also manifest it to you more gloriously than ever before.

The other thing you must keep in view is the purpose for which the Spirit is given. I will put my Spirit within you, and *I will cause you to walk in my statutes and to keep my judgments and do them.* The fullness of the Spirit must be sought and received and kept with the direct aim that you shall now simply and wholly live to do God's will and work upon the earth—yes, only to be able to live like the Lord Jesus, and to say with Him: "Lo! I come . . . to do thy will" (Ps. 40:7, 8; Heb. 10:7). If you cherish this attitude, the fullness of the Spirit may be positively expected. Be full of courage and yield yourself to walk in God's statutes and to keep His judgments and do them, and you may trust God to keep His word that *He will cause you* to keep and do them. He, the living God, will work in you. Even before you are aware how the Spirit is in you, He will enable you to experience the full blessing.

Have you never known the fullness of the Spirit, or have you perhaps been seeking it for a long while without finding it? Here you have at last the sure method of receiving it. Acknowledge your specific sins and make renunciation of them, once and for all, by yielding it up to God. Acknowledge that the Lord Jesus is ready and able to cleanse your heart from its sin; to conquer these sins by His entrance into it, and to set you free; and that His purpose is to do this at once. Take Him now as your Lord, at once and for ever. Then you may be assured that God will put His Spirit within you in a way and a measure and a power of which you have never considered possible. Be assured that He will do it. Allow Him to begin; let Him do it in you now. Amen.

12

How Everything Must Be Given Up for It

"Then shall the Son also himself be subject unto him that put all things under him, that God may be all in all" (1 Cor. 15:28).

When we speak of entire consecration, we are frequently asked what the difference is between the ordinary doctrine of sanctification and the preaching of that gracious work of which we speak. One answer that may be given is that the distinction lies solely in the little word *all*. That word is the secret. The ordinary method of proclaiming the necessity of holiness is true as far as it goes; but sufficient emphasis is not placed on this one point of the *all*. The same word *all* also explains why the fullness of the Spirit is not more widely enjoyed. So long as the *all* of God, of sin, of Christ, of surrender, of the Spirit, and of faith is not fully understood, the soul cannot enjoy *all* that

God desires to give and be, *all* that God would have it be.
In this last chapter let us consider the full Pentecostal
blessing from this standpoint. Let us do this in a spirit of
humble waiting on God, and with the prayer that He would
fully expose to us where the evil lies and what the remedy
is, that we shall be ready to give up everything in order
to receive nothing less than everything.

The All of God

It lies in the very being and nature of God that He
must be all. From Him and through Him and to Him are
all things. As God He is the life of everything: all life is
only the effect of His direct and continuous operation. It
is because all is through Him and from Him that it is also
to Him. Everything that exists is meant to serve only as
a means for the manifestation of the goodness and wisdom
and power of God.

Sin consists in nothing but this, that man determined
to be something and would not suffer God to be everything; and the redemption of Jesus has no other aim than
that God should again become everything in our heart and
life. At the end, even the Son shall be subjected to the
Father that God may be all in all. Nothing less than this
is what redemption is to secure. Christ himself has shown
in His life what it means to be nothing, and to allow God
to be everything; and as He once lived on the earth, so
does He still live in the hearts of His people. According to
the measure in which they receive and rejoice in the truth
that God is all, will the fullness of the blessing be able to
find its way into their life.

The all of God: that is what we must seek. He must be
everything for us—in His will, His honor, His power. No
movement of our time, no word of our lips, no movement
of our heart, no satisfying of the needs of our physical life
should there be that is not the expression of the will, the
glory, the power of God. Only the man who discerns this

and consents to it, who desires and seeks after it, who believes and appropriates it can rightly understand what the fullness of the Spirit must effect, and why it is necessary that we should forsake everything if we desire to obtain it. God must be not merely *something*, not merely *much,* but literally, *all.*

The All of Sin

What is sin? It is the absence of God; separation from God. Where man is guided by his own will, his own honor, his own power; where the will, the honor, the operation of God are not manifested, there sin must be at work. Sin is death and misery only because it is a turning away from God to the creature.

Sin may not exist in man along with other things that are good. No: as God was once everything, so has sin in fallen man become everything. It now dominates and penetrates his whole being, even as God should have been allowed to do. His nature in every part is corrupt. We still have our natural existence in God, and doubtless with not a few good inclinations in nature and character, just as these are to be found in the lower creatures. But of what is *good* in the spiritual and heavenly sense of the word, of what is done out of inward harmony with God or the direction of His Spirit—of all this there is nothing that has its origin in His nature. All is in sin and under the influence of sin.

The all of sin: some small measure of the knowledge of this fact was necessary even at the time of conversion. This, however, was still very imperfect. If a Christian is to make progress and become fully convinced of the necessity of being filled with the Spirit, his eyes must be opened to the extent that sin dominates within him. Everything in him is tainted with sin, his will, his power, his heart; and therefore the omnipotence of God must take in hand the renewal of everything by the Holy Spirit. Man is utterly impotent to that which is good in the highest sense: he can do no more of what is good than what the Spirit actually works in him at any moment. He learns also to see the *all of sin* just as distinctly in the world around him; for the fairest, the most useful, and the most legitimate possessions or enjoyment are all under the power of sin. Everything must be sacrificed and given over to death: the *all of God* must expel the *all of sin*. God must again live wholly and entirely within us, and take inwardly and continously the place which sin usurped. He that desires this change will rightly understand and desire the fullness of the Spirit, and as he believes will certainly receive it.

The All of Christ

The Son is the revelation of the Father: the *all of God* is exhibited to our view and made accessible to us in the Son. On this account the *all of Christ* is just as necessary and infinite as that of God. Christ is God come upon the earth to undo the *all of sin,* to win back and restore in man the lost *all of God*. To this end we must know thoroughly the *all of Christ*.

The idea which most believers have of the *all of Christ* is that He alone does everything in the atonement and the forgiveness of sin. This is indeed the glorious beginning of His redemptive work, but still only the beginning. God has given in Him all that we have need of: life and all grace. Christ himself desires to be our life and strength, the Indweller of our heart, who animates that heart and makes it what it ought to be before God. To know the *all of Christ*, and to understand how intensely and how completely and how really Christ is prepared to be everything in us, is the secret of true sanctification. He that discerns the will of God in this principle and from the heart yields himself to its operation has found the pathway to the full blessing of Pentecost.

The all of Christ. Acknowledge this in humble, joyful thanksgiving: confess that everything has been given by God in Him. Receive with firm confidence the fact that Christ is all and the promise that He will work all, yes, *all,* in you. Consent from the heart that this must be so, and confirm it by laying everything at His feet and offering it up to Him. The two things go together: let Him be and do all; let Him reign and rule over all. Let there be nothing in which He does not rule and operate. It is not impossible for you to accomplish this change. Let Him be everything; let Him have everything, in order that by His almighty energy He may fill everything with himself.

The All of Surrender

Leave all, sell all, forsake all—that was the Lord's requirement when He was here on earth; the requirement is still in force.

The discernment of the fact that Christ is all leads to the acknowledgment that He must have all. The chief hindrance in the Christian life is that, because men do not believe that Christ is all, they consequently never think of the necessity of giving Him all.

Everything must be given to Him because everything is under sin. He cannot cleanse and keep a thing when it is not so yielded up to Him that He can take full possession of it and fill it. All must be given up to Him because He alone can bring the *all of God* to its rightful supremacy within us. Even what appears useful or lawful or innocent becomes defiled by the stain of our selfishness when it is held fast in our own possession and for our own enjoyment. We must surrender it into the hands and the power of Christ: only there can it be sanctified.

The all of surrender: Oh, it is because believers are so ignorant of the requirement that all their praying and hearing avail so little. If you are really prepared to turn to God for the fullness of the Spirit; if you have turned to

Christ to have your heart purified and kept pure; then be assured that it is your blessed privilege to regard and deal with everything—everything that you have to strive for or do as given up to Him. The *all of surrender* will be the measure of your experience of the *all of Christ*. In a preceding chapter we have seen that surrender may be carried out at once and as a whole; let us not simply read and think of this, but actually do it. Yes: this very day, let the *all of Christ* be the power of a surrender on our part that shall be immediate, complete, and everlasting.

The All of the Spirit

The *all of God* and the *all of Christ* demand as a necessary consequence the *all of the Spirit*. It is the work of the Spirit to glorify the Son as dwelling in us, and by Him to reveal the Father; how can He do this if He himself is not *all* and has not *all* and does not possess and penetrate *all* with His own power? To be filled with that Spirit, to let the Spirit have *all*, is indispensable to a true, healthy Christian life.

It is a source of great loss in the life of Christendom that the truth is not discerned, that the Three-One God must have *all*. Even the believer often makes it his very first aim to find out what he is and what he desires, what pleases him and makes him happy. Then he brings in God in the second place to secure this happiness. The claim of God is not the primary or main consideration. He does not discern that God must have him at His disposal even in the most trivial details of his life to manifest His divine glory in him. He is not aware that this entire filling with the will and the operation of God would prove to be his highest happiness. He does not know that the very same Christ who once lived upon the earth as the obedient, lowly Servant of God, entirely surrendered to the will of the Father, is prepared to abide and work in like manner in his heart and life now. It is on this account that he can never fully comprehend how necessary it is that the Spirit must be all and must fill him completely.

If these thoughts have had any influence on you, allow yourself to be brought without delay to the acknowledgment that the Spirit must be all in you. Say from the heart: "I am not at liberty to make any, even the least, exception: the Spirit must have all." Then add to this confession the simple thought that Christ has come to restore the *all of God*; that the Spirit is given to reveal the *all of Christ* within us, so that God may again be *all*; that the love of the Father is eagerly longing to secure again His own supreme place with us; and then your heart will be filled with the sure confidence that the Father actually gives you the fullness of the Spirit.

The All of Faith

"*All things* are possible to him that believeth." "What things soever ye desire, when ye pray, believe that ye receive them, and ye shall have them" (Mark 11:24). The preceding sections of this chapter have taught us to understand why it is that faith is all. It is because God is all. It is because man apart from God is nothing, and thus has nothing good in him except that capacity for receiving God. When he becomes a believer, that which God reveals becomes of itself a heavenly light that illumines. He sees then what God is prepared to be for him; he keeps his soul silent before God and open to God, and gives God the opportunity of working all by the Spirit. The more unceasingly and undividedly he believes, the more fully can the *all of God and Christ* prevail and work in him.

The all of faith. How little it is understood in the Church that the only thing I have to do is to keep my soul in its unceasing nothingness and dependence upon God, that He may be free to work in me; that faith as the willing acceptance and expectation of God's working receives all and can achieve all. Every glance at my own impotence or sin, every glance at the promise of God and His power to fulfill it must rouse me to the gladness of faith, to the willing, cheerful acknowledgment that God is able to work all, to the assurance that He will do it.

Let such a faith, as the act of a moment, look upon Christ even now and move you on the one hand to make renunciation of every known sin, and on the other to receive Him as One who purifies you, who keeps you, who dwells in your heart. Oh, that faith might receive the *all of Christ* and take Him with *all* that He is! Oh, that your faith might then see that the *all of the Spirit* is your rightful heritage, and that your hope is sure that the full blessing has been bestowed upon you by God himself, and will be revealed in you!

If the *all of God,* the *all of Christ*, the *all of the Spirit* be so immeasurable; if the dominion and power of the terrible *all of sin* be so unlimited; if the *all of your surrender* to God and your decision to live wholly for Him be also so real, then let your faith in what God will do for you be also unlimited. "He that believeth in me, out of his heart shall flow rivers of living water."

Before concluding this book, let me press on your heart one thing. There is something that can be done *today*. As the Holy Spirit saith: "Today, if ye will hear his voice, harden not your heart" (Ps. 95:7; Heb. 3:15). I cannot promise that you shall immediately overflow with the light and joy of the Holy Spirit. I do not promise you that you will instantly feel very holy and truly blessed. But what can take place is this: today you may receive Christ as One who purifies you and baptizes and fills with the Spirit. Yes, today you may surrender your whole being to Him to be wholly under the mastery of the Spirit. Today you may appropriate the *all of the Spirit* as your personal possession. Today you may submit to the requirement of the *all of faith* and begin to live only and wholly in the faith of what Christ will do in you through the Spirit. This you may do; this you should do. Kneel at the mercy seat and do it. Read once more the earlier chapter with its directions as to what Christ is prepared to do, and surrender yourself this very hour as an empty vessel to be filled with the Spirit, that your whole life may be lived under the leading of the Spirit. In His own time God will certainly accomplish it in you.

There is also something, however, that He on His part is prepared to do. Today He is ready to give you the assurance that He accepts your surrender and to seal on your heart the conviction that the fullness of the Spirit belongs to you. Oh, wait upon Him to give you this today!

Believer, please listen to my last words. The *all of God* summons you. The *all of sin* summons you. The *all of Christ* summons you. The *all of surrender* summons you. The *all of the Spirit,* His indispensableness and His glory, summons you. The *all of faith* summons you. Come and let the love of God conquer you. Come and let the glorious salvation master you. Do not refuse the glorious tidings that the triune God, with all that He is, is prepared to be your *all*; but be silent and listen to it until your soul becomes constrained to give the answer, "Even in me God shall be all." Take Christ anew today as One who has given His life that God may be all, and yield your life for this supreme end. God will fill you with His Holy Spirit. Amen.